Egypt in the Era of
Hosni Mubarak
1981–2011

Egypt in the Era of Hosni Mubarak
1981–2011

Galal Amin

The American University in Cairo Press
Cairo New York

Copyright © 2011 by
The American University in Cairo Press
113 Sharia Kasr el Aini, Cairo, Egypt
420 Fifth Avenue, New York, NY 10018
www.aucpress.com

First paperback edition 2012

Dar el Kutub No. 2255/12
ISBN 978 977 416 567 2

Dar el Kutub Cataloging-in-Publication Data

Amin, Galal
    Egypt in the Era of Hosni Mubarak: 1981-2011/ Galal Amin; Translated by David Wilmsen.—Cairo:
The American University in Cairo Press, 2012
    p.   cm.
    ISBN 978 977 416 567 2
    1. Egypt-History-1981 I. Wilmsen, David (Tr.)   II. Title
    962.055

1 2 3 4 5   16 15 14 13 12

Designed by Fatiha Bouzidi
Printed in Egypt

Contents

Introduction   1

1 The Soft State   7

2 Corruption   21

3 The Economy   45

4 The Poor   65

5 The Pashas   81

6 The Middle Class   85

7 The Intellectuals   101

8 The Press   111

9 Religious Discourse   121

10 Alienation   133

11 Mubarak's Successor   147

12 Egypt and the Arabs   159

13 Egypt and the United States   167

Introduction

On Tuesday 25 January 2011, hundreds of thousands of Egyptians took to the streets demanding the immediate resignation of President Hosni Mubarak. Demonstrations took place in almost every major city in Egypt and were not confined to the underprivileged classes. They included a large number of highly educated members of the upper and lower middle classes and an unprecedented number of women, of all classes, some of whom came to the streets carrying their young children on their shoulders.

This 'revolution,' which undoubtedly deserves the name, took the world and even the Egyptians themselves by surprise, for it was probably unprecedented in scale in Egyptian history, and there had been no early signs that an event of this magnitude would take place. There were also, surprisingly, no obvious leaders. Contrary to the analysis of foreign commentators on the Egyptian political scene, it was neither led by religious fundamentalists (who were virtually absent from the scene) nor instigated by a hungry mob demanding cheaper food. The slogans were almost completely secular and emphasized the demand for political freedom and respect for human dignity.

Within less than a week, the demonstrators achieved some important gains, including the dismissal or resignation of some of the most unpopular members of the ruling elite. When these concessions proved insufficient, the president announced that he was not going to seek another term of office when the present one elapsed in September 2011. Two days later the newly appointed vice president announced that the president's son, Gamal Mubarak, widely seen as being groomed by his father to succeed him, would no longer be standing for election as president.

On the afternoon of Thursday 10 February, a strong feeling of optimism spread throughout the country following an official announcement that the president was about to make a new address to the nation. Everyone expected his resignation, but the president proved resilient for a little while longer. When he did speak just over an hour before midnight, all he offered was the delegation of some of his powers to his newly appointed vice president but said that he would remain as president until the next elections to be held in September, promising some more reforms in the meantime. The protestors were incensed, with hundreds of thousands gathering in the streets the following day, and starting a march toward the presidential palace determined to bring him down by force. This proved sufficient to force the president to resign. At 6:00 p.m. on the same day, Friday 11 February, the vice president announced in a television address that the president had stepped down and handed power to the Egyptian Armed Forces.

A feeling of euphoria spread throughout the country on hearing the news that the president had stepped down. Egyptians spent the night dancing and singing in the streets, celebrating the end of a regime that, even if a few found it useful for their own purposes, very few really liked and hardly anybody respected.

Even before this dramatic turn of events, it was obvious that the time had come to take a comprehensive look at the whole era of President Mubarak's rule. Almost thirty years have passed since he took office, a long time by any measure. Mubarak came to power when President Reagan had been in office for less than a year in the United States, and Mrs. Thatcher had been prime minister in the United Kingdom for only two years; that is, before neoliberal economic policies had yet to take hold. The Soviet Union was still very much alive and we had not yet heard of Gorbachev or perestroika, let alone the fall of the Berlin Wall and the collapse of one socialist state after another, including the Soviet Union itself.

It was during the Mubarak era that Saddam Hussein attacked the new Islamic regime in Iran, followed by his attack on Kuwait. The United States turned from being a friend of Saddam Hussein to an enemy, also with President Mubarak still in power. When Mubarak became president, the Lebanese civil war was still blazing, King Hussein ruled Jordan, and Hafez al-Assad was president of Syria. Then the events of 11 September 2001 occurred, and Mubarak was still in power to witness the declaration of the so-called War on Terror and the finger of blame and suspicion being directed against Arabs and Muslims. Presidents Ronald Reagan, George H.W. Bush, Bill Clinton, and George W. Bush came and went, while Mubarak continued fixed in place. Presidents and kings come and go, all except for President Mubarak. What a man!

Yet even before the events of January/February 2011, there were many signs that Mubarak's era was nearing its end. Having completed his eighty-third year, the president was already showing signs of age, but there were also signs that preparations were being made for the transition of real power without this being officially declared. Perhaps the formation of the Ahmed Nazif government in the summer of 2004 while President Mubarak was undergoing medical treatment in Germany marked the beginning of this transition.

What better time, then, than the present to look back on the entire era of Mubarak's rule?

President Anwar Sadat left a very heavy burden to his vice president in 1981, both economic and political. On the economic side, Sadat left a huge foreign debt, the likes of which Egypt had not seen before, not even in the days of Khedive Ismail a hundred years before. He also left a high rate of inflation, which was unprecedented in Egypt's modern history, and an economy suffering from what economists call severe 'structural imbalances,' meaning an imbalance in the structure of gross national product, of the labor force, and of exports. This meant, among other things, an economic structure which was very vulnerable to external shocks and incapable of providing well-paid jobs to the greater part of the workforce.

While it is true that there was a high rate of growth in national income during the second half of Sadat's reign, this was due not so much to an increase in domestic production as it was to the high level of migration of labor to the Gulf states, the reopening of the Suez Canal, and a rise in tourism. The growth of these types of income is hardly a reflection of increased production at home and, hence, they are extremely sensitive to political and economic developments in the region, and are, for this reason, exposed to the risk of sudden decline.

Sadat's political legacy was not much better. Mubarak was to inherit a population containing large sections of angry people, as evidenced by the thousands of political prisoners arrested just one month before Sadat was assassinated. Those arrested were of all political colors: Muslims and Christians (including Coptic Pope Shenouda); leftists and Marxists;

Nasserists, Wafdists, and independents; and men along with women. Among them were some prominent persons: Muhammad Hassanein Heikal (Nasserist), Fuad Serag al-Din (Wafdist), Fathi Radwan (nationalist), and Hilmi Murad (independent socialist), as well as the poet Ahmad Fuad Nigm, the musician Sheikh Imam, the Islamist Safinaz Kadhem, and the feminist Nawal El Saadawi.

All opposition newspapers had been closed at the time of Sadat's assassination, but he left behind a well-organized Islamic movement; so well-organized in fact that its partisans were able to kill the president while he was standing amid his army. Sadat was largely responsible for the growth and strengthening of these Islamic groups in the belief that they would support him in his campaign against his leftist opponents; but at the same time he fostered their disenchantment by his signing a peace agreement with Israel in 1979.

What happened to this legacy in the age of Mubarak?

Egyptians had a very short honeymoon with Mubarak, which was perhaps the result of the advice given to him to calm things down after Sadat's assassination by trying to placate the various opposition groups. The new president would invariably answer the foreign correspondents pressing him with the question of whether he intended to apply the same policies of Sadat or whether he would embark upon a new set of policies by smiling broadly and announcing, "My name is Hosni Mubarak!" While it was not a particularly profound reply, reporters and correspondents seemed to take it as an answer showing rare wit, and it would always elicit a laugh. This encouraged the president to keep repeating it. In any event, the president was soon persuaded, after this short honeymoon, to deal passively with the legacy of Sadat, leaving all major decisions (and most of the minor ones as well) in the hands of an alliance of outside and domestic power interests, who found it easy to impose their will on the president.

But let us begin with the honeymoon. A few weeks after the assassination of Sadat, the president took the very promising step of releasing all prominent political prisoners and receiving them in honor at one of his presidential palaces, as if he were apologizing for the uncivilized behavior of his predecessor. Along with this was his decision not to engage in any of the activities that had so annoyed Egyptians under Sadat, such as the constant public appearances of the First Lady and the frequent publication of her photographs in the newspapers. The title of 'First Lady' was completely new to Egyptians at the time: they had never heard it in the Nasser era, or even under the monarchy. So, too, did the new president refrain from referring in public to members of the opposition in insulting terms, as Sadat had been accustomed to do. For example, Sadat had said of the popular preacher Sheikh Kishk that he had been "thrown in prison like a dog," and had called the prominent Egyptian writer and thinker Tawfiq al-Hakim a "charlatan," simply for his having signed a petition calling for action toward the liberation of Sinai. Sadat's outbursts had also included describing his form of democracy as "democracy with fangs" and threatening the opposition not only with prison but also with "annihilation." The new president refrained from using this type of language and appeared to be a very diplomatic president by comparison, and it also appeared as if the new First Lady would adopt an entirely different style from that of her predecessor.

In February 1982, another felicitous step was taken that inspired hope in the hearts of Egyptian economists that genuine economic reform was about to begin. This was when President Mubarak invited some of the most prominent of Egyptian economists, of all different political orientations, to a conference to discuss the deteriorating condition of the Egyptian economy and to suggest ways of getting out of it. All of them were able to express what was on their minds in a manner unknown in the previous twenty years, and which we have not seen since. Looking back on that conference one would be amazed at the ease with which those economists from differing schools of thought could arrive at agreement on solutions for Egypt's pressing economic problems. This showed once again that what had hindered the nation's economic progress were nothing other than bad faith and the triumph of private over public interests.

This was accompanied by a return of the opposition press, and, indeed, the government press was now permitted a freedom it had not enjoyed since the 1952 revolution. Egyptian intellectuals witnessed a golden age of freedom of expression and criticism that engendered among them a feeling of optimism for what political life in Egypt might become. Writers whom Sadat had attacked resumed their writing. Fathi Radwan and Hilmi Murad shone forth once more from the pages of the leftist paper *al-Sha'b*, and Philip Jalab and Salah Eissa in the socialist *al-Ahali*; novelist and playwright Yusuf Idris wrote in *al-Ahram*, and Salah Hafez in *al-Akhbar*. Prominent writers who had suffered under Sadat and despaired of his policies came back from abroad after a long absence. Ahmad Bahaa al-Din came back from Kuwait; Mahmoud Amin al-Alim and 'Abd al-Mu'ti Higazi from France; and even the famous Marxist thinker Samir Amin, who had not been back since 1959 when he had left fleeing arrest, was preparing to return soon to Egypt.

I, too, fell victim to this optimism, and began publishing articles in the magazine *al-Ahram Economic Weekly*. During that short honeymoon the then-editor Dr. Lutfi 'Abd al-Azim turned this magazine into a forum for various points of view. In my articles I was trying to assess the thirty years that had passed since the revolution. So it was that one day I was startled to hear 'Abd al-Azim sadly telling me that a leading nationalist journalist had advised him not to go too far with his optimism, for the situation was still far from becoming clear. So, too, had a prominent politician declared to him that there were signs that a 'mafia' had succeeded in asserting its dominance over Mubarak after persuading him that he should declare himself the president of the ruling party, and not be independent of and above all parties.

Sure enough, the sky began to darken before a single year had passed since Mubarak's ascension to the presidency, and, little by little, we began to despair of any real political or economic change occurring. Then we could gradually sense that a powerful alliance between certain domestic and foreign interests had been formed and dictated all the major decisions, from foreign policy to Arab politics, to the stance toward Israel, and to domestic economic policy. The way the new regime reacted to the recommendations of the economic conference should have given us a portent of things to come. For, after hearing the recommendations of the economic experts and receiving their reports, the ruling party offered sincere thanks to them all and sent them away with the promise that it would form committees to turn all of the recommendations into workable policy. We heard nothing more about new committees or any further meetings of economic experts.

What did happen to the economy, politics, and society in Egypt during the succeeding twenty-seven years is the question that this book will attempt to answer. Nevertheless, while writing many of the chapters, I have found it useful to begin by referring to conditions prevailing before President Mubarak assumed his rule, sometimes going as far back as the time before the revolution, whenever I felt that the contrast would shed more light on the characteristics of the Mubarak era.

1

The Soft State

1

About fifty years ago, when I, together with several other Egyptians who were sent to study economics abroad on state-sponsored fellowships, was trying to discover the secrets of economic development, there were three or four writers who enjoyed our especial reverence and respect. We would snatch up and devour anything they wrote, considering it the last word on the subject of development and backwardness. One of those names, whose penetrating insights and broad horizon distinguished him from most economists, was the Swedish economist and sociologist Karl Gunnar Myrdal. He was one of the last of a generation marked by broad learning and erudition, who could combine a knowledge of economics with politics and sociology, and who refused to reduce economics to a branch of applied mathematics. He would say, "there are no such things as an economic problem, a sociological problem, or a political problem; there are just problems, and they are complex."

In 1968 Professor Myrdal published his book *The Asian Drama: An Inquiry into the Poverty of Nations*, and students of development devoured it with enthusiasm, comparing it with Adam Smith's *An Inquiry into the Nature and Causes of the Wealth of Nations* (which the title of the book invites). I mention Myrdal here particularly because of a theory of his which is stated in this book and expanded in another, released in 1970:[1]

the theory of the 'soft state.' In Myrdal's view, many Third World countries suffer under the yoke of what he calls the soft state, and this could be the clue to some of their greatest afflictions and one of the main reasons for the persistence of their poverty and backwardness.

A soft state is a state that passes laws but does not enforce them. The elites can afford to ignore the law because their power protects them from it, while others pay bribes to work round it. Everything is up for sale, be it building permits for illegal construction, licenses to import illicit goods, or underhand tax rebates and deferrals. The rules are made to be broken and to enrich those who break them, and taxes are often evaded. People clamor for positions of influence so that they may turn them to personal gain. Favors are sold or dispensed to protégés, relatives, and sycophants. Travel grants and foreign currency are handed out to those in power and to those close to them. Token-interest bank loans are granted to the non-creditworthy and then the interest payments are waived, and even the principal may not be repaid since the borrowers are often allowed to leave the country and are never forced to repay what they had borrowed.

In the soft state, then, corruption is generalized and the payment of bribes is widespread; the weakness of the state encourages corruption, and the spread of corruption further weakens the state. Corruption spreads from the executive power to the legislative, and from there to the judiciary. To be sure, some corruption exists in one form or another in all countries, but under the soft state it becomes a way of life.

Myrdal provides a pure class-based interpretation of the soft state: the power that the upper class enjoys enables it to enforce its will upon all other segments of society. The members of this class do not feel as loyal to their country as they do to their families, clans, and clients. If they pass laws, it is to give the appearance of justice and democracy; but they retain full freedom of action in enforcing those laws that redound to their own interests and ignoring those that do not.

Myrdal also points out that there appears to be tacit agreement among writers on development issues to keep quiet about the phenomenon of the soft state. Even if they bring it up and scorn it in private conversations, they do not write about it. International agencies do not even come near the subject in their reports and analyses. There are many reasons for maintaining this silence, which we do not need to go into here, and which discerning readers can deduce for themselves.

When we read what Myrdal wrote at the end of the 1960s, it never occurred to us that his ideas might apply to Egypt; for in those days Egypt was far from being a soft state. We had many problems, but this was not one of them. Of course, there was some corruption and bribery, and some cases of abuse of executive power, but none of these amounted to a way of life in the Egypt of the 1960s. Better examples of what Myrdal was talking about were to be found in South Asia, Latin America, and some of the newly independent African states.

I, myself, came across an example of the soft state when I lived for a few months in Lebanon at the beginning of the 1970s, before the civil war broke out. There I saw for myself much of what Myrdal was talking about, even though (or perhaps because of it) Lebanon was a preferred locale for international corporations and foreign banks. Sadat's rule in Egypt was just beginning, and life in Egypt began year by year to assume a closer and closer resemblance to that in Lebanon. Little by little the government began to back away from its traditional duties, from maintaining security to collecting the trash, from supplying clean water to disposing of sewage, from building new schools to preserving the archaeological heritage, and on and on. Gradually, Egypt was transformed into a soft state. The authority of government ministers dwindled and a new type of government employee appeared who went to work in government offices in the morning and traded in currencies in the evening. Almost every service became subject to negotiation, and getting by depended upon cunning. Despite all of that, by the end of the 1970s the situation had still not reached the same extreme as it had in Lebanon before the civil war, and the Lebanese model had not yet been fully realized in Egypt.

Now that thirty years have passed, we suddenly see that life in Egypt has almost become a copy of life in Lebanon as it was forty years ago. Right from the beginning of the Mubarak era every new day has brought us fresh evidence of the Egyptian soft state. The era began with the attack on the Sabra and Shatila refugee camps in Beirut, which Egypt witnessed as a bystander. Then came the *Achille Lauro* incident and the hijacking of an Egyptian plane in 1986, with no appreciable response from the Egyptian state. Later, the *Salem Express* sank, and the government undertook a surprisingly lax operation for rescuing the survivors. There then followed a shocking scandal involving the minister of petroleum, which ended with his leaving office without being put on trial. Next came the scandal of what were called the 'Islamic Investment Companies,' in which most of the perpetrators managed to slip out of the country. Soon after, the bodies of Egyptians began arriving home from Iraq by the plane-load. Although stories of how they had been shot down in the streets of Baghdad abounded, the Egyptian government released statements exonerating the 'sister' government of Iraq of any responsibility (this, just a few years before Saddam Hussein's government was suddenly transformed into the arch-enemy). Then, after the Gulf War of 1991, half a million Egyptian workers came home from the Gulf to join the ranks of the unemployed in Egypt, and the government did nothing to help them. When the papers published stories about the hundreds of poor in Egypt resorting to selling their kidneys to rich patients from the Gulf and other countries, the government did not stir to prevent them from selling their organs. At the same time, we began to hear stories about mass cheating in school examinations, wherein parents would broadcast by loudspeaker the correct answers to their children in the exam rooms, right under the nose of the state, as if it were powerless to scare them off. Or we heard about a girl attacked by four young men in Ataba Square with no one stopping them except a lone policeman who happened to be passing by and who grabbed one of them and asked the crowd to hold the assailant while he went after the others. All of this notwithstanding, the look of an ordinary policeman in the streets of Cairo would immediately indicate the condition into which the prestige of the state had descended: a fearful, half-starved youth, an ill-fitting uniform hanging from his emaciated frame, without the ability to respond to the insults directed at him from the rich, looking longingly after the charity they might hand out to him.

One day in 1992 an earthquake struck, lasting no more than forty seconds and of an intensity that the Japanese might consider child's play, and suddenly the whole Egyptian government almost collapsed to the ground under the weight of its own weakness. In a single instant it became clear to all the number of buildings constructed against code with no accountability to anyone, the number of extra floors that should have been removed but were not, the heritage buildings needing renovation that had not been renovated, and the schools that should have been condemned long ago into which students were still permitted to enter. So, too, were revealed the types of governors in place who did not see it within their mandate to speak to their constituents and so failed to inform them of what was happening, and the number of members of the local parliaments who remained in Cairo close to the ministries so as to look after the self-interests. What also came to light was the mad speed with ...., for instance, a certain woman owning apartment buildings in Heliopolis could obtain building permits that never would have been granted in the first place except under a soft state. The woman explained the ease with which she obtained them saying, "I know quite well how the game is played in Egypt." The earthquake revealed, in a way that could leave no doubt, the extent of governmental bias toward the inhabitants of Cairo over the other regions of Egypt: almost all beneficiaries of the soft state live in Cairo.

The soft state came to Egypt about thirty-five years ago. We are accustomed to saying that what happened then was the implementation of the *infitah*, that is, the introduction of Open Door liberal economic policies initiated by Sadat, and we often ascribe many of the unfortunate phenomena of the type I have mentioned to the policies of the *infitah*. Some have pointed out that the issue is not simply that of the implementation of liberal policies, rather it is the specific types of policies. Prominent journalist Ahmad Bahaa al-Din has called this "helter-skelter" liberalization; that is, liberalization without regulation or legal underpinning. Nevertheless, perhaps the idea of Myrdal's 'soft state' is more useful in specifying what happened in Egypt a third of a century ago, and which persists to the present day. For the truth is that what happened was not what is generally understood to be economic liberalization, that is, the government relinquishing its control of economic activities that could be undertaken by private firms and instead focusing on basic infrastructure, preserving order, and the rule of law. Instead, the state embarked upon many purely commercial projects, like building summer vacation villas for the elite along the northern seacoast, while neglecting its traditional responsibilities of maintaining the infrastructure, schools, hospitals, roadways, archaeological sites, and so on. What happened was not opening the door wide to competition and cancelling protection for local producers. Rather, it was opening the door to imports—or closing it, imposing protection—or lifting it, as suited the interests of a powerful elite.

Egyptians have always been better off under a strong state. When the Egyptian state is strong, the economy flourishes, taxes are collected, and the state launches development projects and provides public services, creates jobs, and furnishes the poor with a safety net. When the state is weak, taxes are not collected, people are left to break the law, they lose respect for the police, traffic laws are flouted, and security is lax.

This may be true of many other countries as well, but not all. For example, in Lebanon, the economy seems to flourish more under a weak state, and the Arab countries of North Africa seem to be less in need of a strong government than Egypt. The Americans seem by nature to abhor a strong state and pride themselves in one that leaves them alone. With Egypt, however, whether we look to its recent history, to the medieval era, or to ancient times, we find general prosperity coinciding with the existence of a strong state.

Many writers see this as a result of Egypt's complete reliance on the Nile for survival, which demands the constant attention of a strong centralized state. When the water supply is short, the government must intervene to ensure its equitable distribution; and when it is abundant, the state must intervene to protect the land and its inhabitants from overflooding. One may also add the high population density along the banks of the Nile; for the larger the population density, the greater the need for a strong nation.

It is interesting to note that Napoleon, in exile on St Helena, writes in his memoirs that he knows of no other country in the world in need of a strong central government to the degree that Egypt does.[2] As such, Egypt was bound to pay more dearly than many other countries for the weakening of the state that began in the 1970s.

The question is, "What gave rise to the soft state in Egypt about a third of a century ago, that is, toward the middle of the Sadat era, after twenty years of a strong state under Nasser; and what factors led to increased softness in the Mubarak era, especially during the last twenty years?"

2

Toward the beginning of the 1970s, a powerful wind began to blow through the world, which, in line with prevalent terminology, we might call the 'wind of globalization.' This was, of course, not the first gust of globalization; the classic and modern examples of colonialism are also manifestations of globalization. Colonialism brings far countries close, widens markets, and supplies raw materials from the farthest corners of the earth. In other words, it cuts short the distances traveled by goods, capital, and people—and even ideas and lifestyles. Nevertheless, whereas the earlier waves of globalization mainly took the form of the occupation by one nation's armies of the lands of another nation, the current wave, which began in the last third of the twentieth century, is characterized by what we might call the 'gradual dissolution of the state.' Hidden behind these earlier and later waves of globalization have always been economic factors; but while economic interests were at one time best served by military occupation, these interests are now better served by the dissolution of the state.

The current stage of globalization came at the end of the three decades following the end of the Second World War (1945–75), which were characterized by strong government intervention in society and the economy. I am, of course, not just referring to Egypt here, but to all of the Third World and, indeed, with the necessary qualifications, to the developed world as well. The intervention came in the form of nationalization, creating protective barriers against foreign goods and capital, imposing a minimum wage and social and economic protection measures for workers, price control, high taxes, and a strong trend toward the redistribution of income and wealth.

The current wave of globalization aims at exactly the opposite. It has been brought about by a flood of capital and goods seeking new markets for investment to offset the increasing saturation of the markets and higher wages in the more developed countries, resulting in falling rates of return on investment. This requires markets that are not surrounded by walls of protectionism, new investment opportunities free from state intervention and unencumbered by high taxes, and a cheap labor force with no minimum wage or job protection. If the investment opportunities come in the form of privatization of existing firms, so much the better. Investors save themselves the risk of embarking upon new ventures by putting their hands on fully formed, profitable enterprises ready for sale. Some writers have called this 'accumulation by acquisition' or what we might call the 'sequestration of public property for private use,' which is just the opposite of the 'sequestration of private property for public use.' All of this requires a soft state. The weaker the state, the easier the access to new markets, to new investment opportunities under the easiest of terms, and to cheap labor. If the state is strong, it must be broken up.

This is one of the most important features of the last thirty years, not just in Egypt, but in the whole world. It happened in the Soviet Union, and it led to its fall, and it happened in Eastern Europe, leading to the fall of one communist regime after another. Indeed, it happened in Western Europe as well, with the spread of privatization and steps being taken toward the dismantling of the welfare state. So, too, has it happened in one Third World state after another. As a result, many ordinary citizens in Russia and the rest of Eastern Europe, as well as in many Third World countries and even in the western capitalist countries, came to bear a heavy burden trying to have access to education, health care, and job opportunities. For the same reason, Egyptian citizens came to bear such a heavy burden as well.

3

It is difficult to imagine that the Egyptian state after 1967 could have retained the same strength as it had beforehand. True, the military was successful in crossing into Sinai in the 1973 war, but this military accomplishment was not accompanied by any political achievement. Indeed, Egypt was forced to make various concessions in the agreements with Israel that followed, beginning with the disengagement agreement of 1975 and leading up to the peace agreement of 1979, and these concessions contributed to the further weakening of the Egyptian state. How did this happen?

The United States entered as a party to the agreements for the liberation of the Sinai from Israeli occupation in return for Egypt's submission to American demands. This was sanctified by a huge celebration on the occasion of the visit of President Nixon to Egypt in 1973, as if he were a Roman emperor coming to inspect a costly pearl that had lately been added to his possessions. But this emperor asked for a heavy price: from rearming the Egyptian army with American weaponry to opening the Egyptian economy to western capital and goods, and gradually distancing Egypt from the Arab region, especially, of course, with respect to Egypt's relationship with Israel.

Accepting all this meant explicit submission on Egypt's part to foreign will, namely the will of the United States, the will of Israel, and the will of foreign capital. This, in turn, has led to the weakening of the Egyptian state toward other Arab states. As the United States and Israel have their own ambitions and interests in other Arab countries, revolving around the establishment of close relations between them and Israel, and the widening of economic liberalization to encompass the entire Arab region, they required, and, indeed, received, Egypt's services in all of these directions. The other Arab states gradually discovered that they had lost Egypt as a leader, mentor, and mediator in inter-Arab conflicts. Thus, just as the Egyptian state has become subservient in its relationships with the United States, Israel, and foreign capital, so it has become in its relationships with other Arab states as well.

This weakness was also bound to be reflected in the relationship between the Egyptian state and the Egyptian people. The new relationships that emerged between Egypt and the United States, Israel, and foreign capital required a new type of person to take up high government posts as ministers and prime ministers. Even if some of them had also served in the 1950s and 1960s, they had to be ready to change their skin.

For one thing, they had to be people with no resentment toward American policies in the region, and if they also had a natural weakness for the American way of life and liked to distinguish themselves by leading similar lifestyles, so much the better. It was good if they hated anything remotely connected with socialism, and held or displayed a strong faith in the free market and in its power to vouchsafe the best economic results. They also had to be people who did not view Israel with the same resentment as did the general Egyptian public, people who liked to call themselves 'realists' in their readiness to accept Israel as a fact of life, and people who did not empathize too strongly with the plight of the Palestinians, but were ready instead to blame them for their predicament.

One prominent example of the difference between the ruling regime in the 1970s and that of the 1960s is illustrated by the central role played by Othman Ahmad Othman and his company, Arab Contractors, and by his relationship to the state. Under Nasser, Othman, with all of his wealth and power, was more like a government employee taking his orders from the head of state and anxious not to lose favor. Under Sadat, it was as if he had become a partner in the business of government. The close connection between them was cemented by Othman's son marrying into the president's family.

Despite all the manifestations of a soft state that emerged during the 1970s, the second half of the decade saw something of a boom in the economy, with money pouring into Egypt from remittances of Egyptian workers in the Gulf, foreign aid, Suez Canal revenues, oil, and tourism. The resulting increase in the purchasing power for wide segments of the population, even among the poorest Egyptians, helped to conceal, to some extent, the growing weakness of the state. The situation was rather like a weak-willed man of limited means, with a big family, who suddenly inherited a fortune at the unexpected death of a relative, and who could then cover up his lack of any real ability with ostentatious spending.

Emigration itself lessened people's awareness of the weakness of the Egyptian state. It prevented Egyptian émigrés from seeing first-hand the decline in education and other public services, as their children were probably enjoying far better education and medical care in the oil states than they would have received in Egypt. By the mid-1980s, however, Egypt entered a new phase with the ending of the boom that had begun ten years earlier, as the emigration rate slackened and many émigrés returned to Egypt, and when some distance had been gained from the harshness of the Nasserist state. It was natural, therefore, that Egyptians would feel and suffer more from the increasing weakness of the state from then onward.

4

President Nasser had a project. To put this project into effect, he attracted men who believed in his vision or at least professed a belief in it. President Sadat presented the Egyptians with a new vision, quite opposed to that of Nasser, and he in turn attracted men who believed or pretended to believe in his project. For his part, Hosni Mubarak had no project of his own. Instead, he was content to continue without any deviation on the path opened up by Sadat.

Mubarak gave a rather strange explanation for the colorlessness of his regime, saying that he did not subscribe to a policy of "shock therapy." He neither closed the doors of the economy, nor opened them wider. He did not go to war with Israel, nor did he oppose Israeli attacks on other Arab countries.

But, with this kind of regime that Egypt had under Mubarak, a new type of official was needed to fill key positions of state. For, regardless of how one feels about the policies of Nasser or of Sadat, one has to admit that most of the men who surrounded them, whether giving advice or implementing policies, were for the large part political men. Politics ran in their blood, occupied their minds, and governed their behavior. Many of them shared with either of the two presidents his enthusiasm for the policies they were implementing. That began to change gradually in the Mubarak era, until we finally came to see the arrival of ministers or even prime ministers about whom we knew virtually nothing before they assumed their posts. There was no way of knowing beforehand what their policies might be. Indeed, it became quite clear that the prime minister himself did not know exactly what the foreign minister or the ministers of the economy, the interior, or information intended doing. Orders would come from higher up, which in turn came from even higher up. The ministers, for their part, were no closer to having a vision or a blueprint for what they were planning to do than was the prime minister. The minister of education had no policy for education, and the same was true for the ministers of health, housing, and economic planning and development. The same could be said for those running the government newspapers and television.

Indeed, it was notable that many of those who assumed prominent positions over the last twenty years had attained a conspicuously lower level of education than those who had held the same posts during the 1960s and 1970s. Many of them seemed to possess a high degree of social intelligence, had the ability to "juggle an egg and a stone," as the popular expression has it, knew how to play the game to balance effective power among those in higher positions, and they also knew, of course, the best way to get to the heart and mind of the president. They were, nevertheless, little able to go further than this in their understanding of international politics, or in comprehending the full economic or social effects of the Open Door policies.

Those changes that have come about in the type of men surround-ing the president have had a significant effect in weakening the Egyptian state. When one is hardly interested in politics and not particularly well educated or cultured, there remains little more than personal gain as a motivation for involvement. Personal gain for some could simply mean holding high office or enjoying power that one had not previously wielded, but for most of them personal gain comes in the form of material wealth. Such an aim can be realized only under a soft state.

5

Making matters considerably worse in the past twenty years has been the interference of the International Monetary Fund in Egyptian economic policy since 1987, when the government's inability to service its foreign debts on time became apparent. In 1991 Egypt signed the Stabilization and Structural Adjustment agreement with the Fund, which involved gradual government withdrawal from many of the functions that the public had been accustomed to since the 1960s, and expedited the privatization of public sector companies. What had appeared as moderate softness of the state in the 1970s and 1980s burgeoned in these last twenty years.

For example, in the field of education, the 1970s saw the emergence of the problem of private tutoring by school teachers and university professors, although this played a much smaller role then than it does today in the life of millions of Egyptian families, as a result of the increasing loss of state control.

The 1970s also saw the advent of private schools and the reappearance of foreign-language schools, followed by the multiplication of foreign universities in the 1980s. Indeed, western-style education has penetrated state universities with the opening of departments teaching in foreign languages alongside their counterparts teaching in Arabic. This has deepened the split of Egyptian society into two: one part consisting of those who can afford the fees of a private and western-style education, and those who cannot. The government makes a show of supervising what goes on in these schools and universities, but has really very little power (or even inclination) to assert itself.

A similar change occurred in the cultural life of the country. Over the past twenty years the state has reduced the support it had previously given to a national theater, to film production, and to book publishing, leaving a big vacuum to be filled by the private sector, not always with favorable effect. There is nothing objectionable in having a new opera house built with a grant from Japan, but it is very offensive to the eye as well as the heart to see car companies using the entrance of the opera complex as an automobile showroom. Likewise, the Cairo International Book Fair, which had been run by the state since 1969, started in the last few years to be held under the sponsorship of one of the mobile telephone companies, and the lanes of the fairground came to be filled with advertisements for the company. The new management of the fair felt inclined to reduce the number of forums customarily held for discussing matters of general interest to the reading public so as to increase the marketing facilities for private companies.

In the media, the state retained its ownership of the newspapers and magazines it had nationalized in the 1960s and their editors-in-chief remained in place throughout the 1970s along with their notable writers and journalists, most of whom enjoyed the respect of their colleagues and subordinates. Beginning in the 1980s, however, these papers and magazines began to transform themselves little by little into what looked like the private fiefdoms of the chairmen of the boards and the editors-in-chief, who made their fortunes from advertising revenues and from publishing laudatory news and opinions of those in or close to power.

This gradual withdrawal by the state from the areas of education, culture, the media, and other spheres was bound to come at the expense of the poorer classes of society, who found themselves obliged to take up the burden of private education in a desperate attempt to compensate for the decline in the quality of public education, and who found that the right to enjoy high culture and art had become conditional, more than ever, on the ability to pay. They also found themselves increasingly alienated by what they saw on their television screens or read in the so-called 'national' newspapers and magazines.

One cannot follow what has been going on during the last twenty years on all these fronts without recalling the system of 'tax farming' that existed under the Ottomans in the eighteenth century.[3] The Ottoman state, and its governor in Egypt, had reached such a point of weakness that it was incapable of managing public utilities for the general good, or of collecting enough tax revenues to re-invest in the necessary public infrastructure. It therefore ceded the right to collect taxes to some rich individuals who sucked whatever they could out of the people (by force if necessary). This right to act as an intermediary between the people and the state was given for a comparatively small price paid to the governor and the occasional gift sent his way.

2

Corruption

1

Upon hearing the word 'corruption,' what may immediately come to mind is a government employee or official in the central or local government who abdicates the responsibility of performing a task for the public good, in pursuit of private gain. An example of this would be a government employee accepting a bribe in return for disregarding a court order to demolish an apartment building or remove unlicensed floors, for permitting the importation of tainted food products, or for allowing the sale of polluted drinking water, and so on.

The temptation to engage in such acts of corruption can be expected to increase the stronger the desire for the reward and the easier it is to escape the penalty. Under certain social conditions, such as those which prevailed in Egypt during the last two decades, both the desire for the reward and the opportunity to get away with it greatly increased. There was, indeed, corruption under the monarchy, just as there was under Nasser, and it persisted under Sadat as well as under Mubarak; but there are important differences between these eras in the nature and degree of corruption that are worth highlighting.

It is first necessary to distinguish between the first decades of the monarchy in Egypt and its final decade, the 1940s. Perhaps the least amount of corruption that Egypt has known during the last two centuries was in the 1920s and 1930s, that is, the two decades immediately following the 1919 revolution and the introduction of a modern constitution in 1923. Corruption increased and spread during the years of the Second World War and those following it, until the 1952 revolution. It is easy to explain the differences in the scale of corruption between these two periods of the monarchical era.

The men holding high office in the 1920s and 1930s were of a type that is difficult to imagine at present. Some of them had been known for their history of opposition to the British occupation, but the large majority of them were esteemed for distinction in their professions before taking office: a prominent lawyer, a brilliant physician, a talented writer, and so on. Likewise, the great majority of them were members of genuine political parties competing for the chance to rule. What distinguished the parties from each other was not their degree of integrity but their stance toward the British as well as the social class whose interests they were inclined to represent. One may also add the personal inclination of the leaders of these parties toward a greater or lesser degree of demagoguery.

For these reasons, throughout the monarchical era and especially in the 1920s and 1930s, the position of a minister or of a prime minister enjoyed enormous prestige and respect, not just for the wide power of the office, but also for the personalities and history of those who had held such jobs. This was in addition to the prestige enjoyed by the upper classes, to which most of the ministers and prime ministers belonged; a prestige which was derived from their inherited wealth and not just from their ascension to office.

If that was the case for the high officials, what about the impoverished majority of the people? Did not their extreme poverty and the disparity that existed in wealth and income make them more inclined to take bribes? Poverty was indeed severe and the disparities between the classes were indeed wide, but it seems that what is more important than the degree of poverty or of class distinctions in generating corruption is how the people viewed their poverty and these class distinctions.

I can still clearly remember how the poor regarded the rich in pre-revolutionary Egypt, and vice versa. The literature and films of the 1930s and 1940s also give a good idea of the nature of the relations between rich and poor. The picture is that of each of the two classes regarding the other as if it were of a different species. The long history of foreign rule must have played a role, including the lengthy and quite recent history of Turkish rule in Egypt. But there is also the long history of income disparity and of the iron wall that for so long had separated the rich and the poor. All of this must have contributed to the strength of feeling that the poor would forever remain poor and that the rich would likewise remain rich.

Social mobility was exceedingly slow before the revolution of 1952. The few examples of Egyptians rising from the lower to the middle class in the century preceding 1952 were mainly those of a few very talented people who had been given a rare opportunity to gain an education and excel. Even more rarely were those who were lucky in commerce, the largest share of which was reserved for foreigners. Contributing to the slow pace of social mobility were the very low rates of economic development and inflation. In such a climate, the hope for social mobility must wane, but the fear of decline in social status also wanes and the temptation to give or accept bribes fades, as does the desire to approach the ruling elite hoping for some large recompense.

During the 1920s and 1930s there prevailed a strong feeling of patriotism, which helped enforce the resistance to corruption. Such a feeling tends to promote moral commitment, reinforces a sense of obligation to the public interest, and weakens the drive to pursue private gain at any cost. No one can claim that a strong feeling of patriotism prevailed among the great majority of Egyptian peasants before or after 1952, for it is difficult to imagine poverty-stricken peasants, denied the basics of life, being able to share the national aspirations of the time or to appreciate the value of standing against the British occupation. The nationalist movement was not completely absent from the Egyptian countryside, but it did not extend much further than the middle-class agricultural landholders. For the great majority of farm workers and small sharecroppers, the burden of sheer survival was enough to keep them from being committed to any other goal. Nevertheless, it remained true that in the three decades following the 1919 revolution, patriotic sentiments beat powerfully in the hearts of the Egyptian middle classes, both in the countryside and in the cities.

In the first half of the twentieth century the middle class in Egypt possessed some admirable traits that it gradually lost during the second half. The main source of the growth in the size of the middle class in Egypt in the first half of the century was education, with growth in industry, agriculture, and commerce being exceedingly slow, and those engaged in industry or commerce being mainly foreign nationals. What is truly astonishing when one compares the state of education in the first half of the twentieth century to its current state is its high quality in the earlier period at both school and university levels. A high standard of education combined with a strong feeling of patriotism among the middle classes tended to strengthen moral sense and disdain for anything that hinted of corruption.

It was natural that the middle class, enjoying these traits (stability, self-confidence, and a high level of education and morals), would have a more rational understanding of religion, less shaped by superstition and affectation. It was, then, quite possible to reconcile a powerful religious sentiment with a robust sense of patriotism, a very rational view of life, and a great tolerance for the adherents of other religions and for conflicting viewpoints. There did not appear to be any contradiction between a strong sense of belonging to one's own Muslim, or Coptic, community and a deep loyalty to the Egyptian nation; a rational religious viewpoint could accommodate both. An emotional and fanatical view of religion would, however, come to encourage a split between the two loyalties as well as create a wide gulf between strong believers and secularists, and would foster an understanding of religion as encompassing the whole of life and an understanding of politics as nothing more than a certain stance toward religion.

I maintain that the important change that came over the nature of religious discourse during the last three decades of the twentieth century permitted a climate conducive to the increase in corruption rather than closing the door on it. It is a very easy thing to reconcile the practice of corruption with the pretence of religiosity; it is also easy for people to accept bribes or engage in cheating while mouthing religious expressions, whereas it is hard for someone who adheres to the core precepts of religion to do so.

Everything I say here is relative, and is put forward as a way of highlighting the differences between one era and another and not to portray one era rather than another as utterly pure and incorrupt. There is no doubt, for example, that in the years immediately preceding the 1952 revolution the talk of corruption and repeated examples of it gave rise to the catchphrase "fighting corruption" as one of the most important slogans of the Free Officers who staged the revolution. Immediately afterward, revolutionary courts were set up for the trial of those who were deemed to have engaged in corruption. What was happening, then, during the last years of the monarchy in the social and political climate to permit the growth of corruption?

<h1 style="text-align:center">2</h1>

During the ten years immediately preceding the revolution a climate of social tension prevailed in Egypt, unknown during the previous two decades or, for that matter, in the two succeeding decades. One cause was doubtless the Second World War and the attendant change in the international climate, which was in turn reflected in everyday life in Egypt.

The rate of inflation suddenly rose because of the war and increased wartime spending by the British forces in Egypt. With the rise in inflation came unprecedented opportunities for a small section of the population for upward mobility; Egyptians began to joke about "the war rich," and stories went round about some humble trader or other who became a rich big shot by doing business with the British occupation forces, or about some small-time workshop owner who became a millionaire in the space of a few years because of the natural monopoly that the war provided him. The price of agricultural land shot up too because of the rising rate of population growth, with little effort being expended in the reclamation of new land.

Migration to the cities by Egyptians in search of job opportunities increased; but as soon as the war ended unemployment rose because of lax government spending and shrinking of British troop deployment. Social problems manifested themselves much more clearly than they had previously in the 1920s and 1930s: the gap between social classes widened, and poverty was no longer considered an exclusively rural phenomenon, as it had been for centuries. It is interesting to note that the greatest Egyptian author of the day, Taha Hussein, who just before the outbreak of the war wrote a book full of optimism about the future of Egypt, in which he outlined a plan for the development of education and culture (*Mustaqbal al-thaqafa fi Misr* [The Future of Culture in Egypt], 1938), found himself at the end of the 1940s obliged to write about a subject he had never addressed before, namely the distribution of income in a book called *al-Mu'adhdhabun fi-l-ard* (The Afflicted of the Earth, 1948).

The rising expectations caused by greater social mobility and inflation on the one hand and the growing discontent over deteriorating income distribution on the other must have created a greater motivation for people to use special influence to gain upward mobility or at least to prevent downward mobility. But, at the same time, there was a waning of the power of the state—for reasons not unconnected to the war, which allowed those disposed to exercise their influence illegitimately to do so.

From the beginning of the war, the British had begun to apply more and more pressure on the Egyptian state—both the king and the government—than they had done in peacetime. It was unimaginable for the British to permit the king or the Egyptian government to do anything that might weaken their chances of winning the war, even if that meant sending tanks to surround the Abdin Palace, where the king lived, to impose a government which the king did not want (as actually happened on 4 February 1942). Such an employment of naked power by the occupying authority inspired feelings of fear and despair in both the king and the nationalist movement. Adding considerably to the discontent was the fact that at the end of the war the British showed no sign of responding to the national movement's demands for evacuation, and one government after another failed in negotiations with the British or in presenting their case to the United Nations. At the same time, the Islamic movement increased its violence against the state when its members murdered a judge whose ruling angered the Muslim Brotherhood. The state disbanded the organization, which responded by assassinating the prime minister. His successor countered by arranging the assassination of the head of the Brotherhood, and on it went. Meanwhile, the Jews in Palestine announced the founding of the State of Israel, and war in Palestine broke out in 1948 with Egypt entering with an army unprepared for war and returning in defeat. At the same time, Egypt was opened up to a new world in which appeared for the first time seductive American goods, from fast cars to fun films, from nylon shirts to Coca-Cola and Chiclets chewing gum.

In this climate, the royal palace was unsurprisingly stricken with extreme weakness and despair, and so were successive Egyptian governments, each one weaker than its predecessor. Even the most popular political party in Egypt, the Wafd, with its long history of struggle for independence, and headed by leaders famous for their uprightness and incorruptibility, was plagued with debilitating weakness. No wonder that these leaders appeared ready to tolerate corruption to a degree not seen before, and indeed to practice it to an extent unknown in Egypt in the first decades of the century.

People began to tell of corruption in the King's private life, his neglect of his duties and his behavior in a manner unbefitting a monarch, his accepting of bribes from the very rich of Egypt in return for lowering taxes on them, or his granting of generous government financial assistance in return for benefits to himself. Stories about bribes in the form of gambling losses went round, involving some rich fellow going to the Automobile Club (a gentleman's club in downtown Cairo) and deliberately dropping ten or twenty thousand Egyptian pounds in a game with the king in exchange for some government decree in his favor or just in order to gain the title of pasha.

The prominent journalist and writer Ahmad Bahaa al-Din, in his book *Farouk malikan* (Farouk as King) published a few months after the 1952 revolution, wrote that,

> In Europe, agents of the king were concluding deals for faulty weaponry to be shipped to Palestine, where they would explode in the hands of the soldiers bearing them. These heinous deals netted hundreds of thousands of pounds in profit. The minister of war knew about them, as did all ministers, but they kept silent, because the merchant behind the deals was the king. (p. 105)

Bahaa al-Din also relates an interesting story that illustrates the extent of irresponsibility toward the law that the king had reached on the one hand and the weakness that afflicted the largest nationalist party on the other:

> It was logical that these [opposition] newspapers would not limit their campaign to the person of the king and his entourage, instead extending their attacks to the gloomy social situation, the miserable economy, and the unstable state of the nation. The king was alarmed by the extent of the revolutionary fervor that extended right up to the doors of the palace, and he began to pressure the government to impound these newspapers. The government did indeed begin to impound them, whereupon the Council of State would unanimously overturn the government's ruling.

> In September 1951, the king was in Capri when a cabinet session was convened in Alexandria, and Prime Minister Mustafa al-Nahhas[4] entered the hall where the session was being held, visibly upset, and dropped this announcement on the assembled ministers: the king had sent orders calling for a ministerial decree dissolving the Council of

State as punishment for the rulings it had issued and that he was sending the decree already signed from Capri, which the ministers were to
sign as a *fait accompli*. The ministers were stunned. A fierce discussion
ensued among the assembled officials, during which al-Nahhas uttered
not a word. The minister of foreign affairs quickly wrote a note to al-
Nahhas submitting his resignation, saying that he would depart from
the people's government before it ever issued a decree against the
people's interest. Al-Nahhas exploded, beating on the table, roaring,
"So that's it, is it? You want to kill me? You want to be a hero at my
expense?" Knowing al-Nahhas's character, the minister waited until
the storm had blown over and the prime minister had given full vent
to his feelings. Then he began speaking to al-Nahhas with a voice full
of sincerity, justifying his action, "I want to protect you, not kill you."
At that, the assembled ministers were startled to see al-Nahhas begin
to weep. The ministers, considering the storm raging inside al-Nahhas,
the competing considerations pulling him one way and another, and
the fine line he was about to tread between a glorious past and a future
that he was trying to guarantee, and the impotence that had come over
him, rushed to his side like children whose father had become beset by
a crisis and wept. He said, "Ok . . . ok . . . do not resign. And I shall put
the decree into the drawer. I won't sign it . . . ." (pp. 178–82)

These events came about ten months before the revolution, and they
are a good illustration of the climate at the time of the revolution; they
were among the main reasons for the enthusiastic welcome with which
the people received it and the joy they felt, and an important justification
for initiating it in the first place. But the men who staged the revolution
never found it convenient to mention two other things, not at the time of
the revolution and not at any time afterward:

1. That the extent of corruption and disdain for the law exhibited by
the king and his retinue in the 1940s and early 1950s was not characteris-
tic of the climate prevailing in Egypt in the three decades that separated
the revolution of 1919 and the 1952 Nasserist revolution—a climate thor-
oughly conducive to respect for the law, as I have tried to explain.

2. That even in the decade leading up to 1952, corruption was largely
restricted to a very narrow circle: that of the king and his retinue. Outside
of that circle, the Egyptian middle class generally retained its hold on
upstanding morals, honor, and respect for the law. Any deviation from

those values was considered disgraceful in the extreme, enough to ruin the perpetrator's name for good. Away from the king, the prevalent form of corruption was of one of favoritism, in most cases having very little effect on the public good, such as the promotion of an unqualified relative or friend to a higher government post, or providing some financial advantages to a favorite employee at the expense of another more deserving. It was never imagined, for example, throughout the three decades before the 1952 revolution that a university president with no scholarly qualifications and a personality unfit for such a post might actually be appointed, or that a court judgment might be issued against some VIP but never executed. Indeed, even with the king and his court, a reading of the stories of the corruption they engaged in or attempted in their final ten years reveals that almost all of them also involved some honorable person or people inside the government who tried to stop it, very often successfully. Thus the story of al-Nahhas refusing to sign the order dissolving the Council of State was by no means the only one of its kind, and many were the times that the government, even a minority government, refused to submit to the will of the king. The popularity of a man, then, or the backing of the people (as was the case with Mustafa al-Nahhas) were not the only impetus (indeed, perhaps not even the main impetus) causing a minister or prime minister, the head of the privy council or the Council of State, an attorney general or a judge to stand in opposition to the king's will; rather, the main factor was a firm commitment to ethical principles.

Without a doubt, one of the factors that assisted in limiting the extent of corruption before the revolution was the narrow scope of government activity. One would expect that government intervention in every aspect of life, great and small, and the growth in the legal regulation of individual activity would, all things being equal, encourage the spread of corruption. There is also a lot of truth to the saying, "power corrupts, and absolute power corrupts absolutely." Government officials before the revolution had held less power compared to those who came afterward, so the opportunities to exploit their power were necessarily limited. The situation changed after the revolution with the increase in laws and restrictions on individual activities imposed by the new government, in addition to the weakness afflicting the municipalities. For that reason alone, the rise in corruption after the revolution of 1952 could have been expected. Fortunately, in the first fifteen years after the revolution, the prevailing climate was very different from that of the 1940s, and Egyptians enjoyed a period of high integrity among government officials and respect for the law that was not to be seen again in the aftermath of the 1967 defeat. This needs some explanation.

<h1 style="text-align:center">3</h1>

Nasser was certainly a dictator, but he was not corrupt. He lived and died in the same house he had resided in before the revolution. Throughout their lives, he and his wife remained moderate in the way they dressed and conducted their daily life without pomp or luxury, and they died without leaving any wealth to speak of. The few attempts made after Nasser's death to establish that he had left an account in a foreign bank met with abject failure. This asceticism was sure to reflect on the men directly around him, because Nasser would neither imagine nor accept that one of his men might become rich with public money. The fear of their president was enough to curb their selfish ambitions, if they had been unable themselves to resist the temptation of wealth.

A friend of mine working in the Egyptian embassy in Rome in 1959 told me about a time he was assigned as an aide to Sadat on a tour of the streets and shops of Rome, long before Sadat became president. Sadat found a jacket he liked, a very loud green one, which he considered buying, but thought the better of it, uttering a phrase that expressed what Nasser would say if he saw him wearing it. Similarly, in a book published after the death of the two presidents, entitled *Shahid bayna 'asrayn* (Memories of Two Eras), Salah al-Shahid, chief of protocol before and after the revolution, tells how Nasser refused his children electrical toys that other Egyptians were prohibited from acquiring, and of their fear of getting them, to avoid his displeasure. Likewise, the prominent lawyer and writer Fathi Radwan, who also served as minister of culture under Nasser, in his book, *Ithanyn wa-sab'un shahran ma' 'Abd al-Nasser* (Seventy-two Months with 'Abd al-Nasser) paints a clear picture of Nasser's personality as having no weakness for money or the blandishments of a life of ease.

A surprisingly austere life prevailed among the middle class in Egypt in the days of Nasser that someone who did not live through them would find difficult to credit. Stores sold almost nothing but Egyptian-made products, whether clothing, foodstuffs, or furniture. There was practically only one brand of automobile on the streets (the Nasr car, which was assembled in Egypt); refrigerators and kitchen appliances were almost all made by the Egyptian factories of the Ideal appliance company. Egyptians finding a reason to go abroad for work or study might sometimes return with American refrigerators or German washing machines, if they were able to afford the steep duties imposed on the importation of such goods. They would then be regarded by friends and neighbors with awe; indeed, possession of such goods might inspire more embarrassment than pride in the midst of such severe austerity.

Because of this general austerity, there was little opportunity for corruption, and in truth, it rarely amounted to more than such things as some official sneaking a crystal chandelier past customs without paying duties or the head of a food co-operative adding a few frozen chickens to the allotment of another official and delivering them to his house so that he would not have to stand in line like everyone else. That such things in the 1960s were considered very serious examples of corruption is an indication of how limited its extent was in that decade.

This cannot be explained simply by the good example set by the president; rather, it was the general climate that encouraged respect for the law and kept corruption at a low. Many prominent figures and office holders in the public sector behaved very differently under Nasser from the way they did after his death, including Anwar Sadat himself. During the 1960s, they were dedicated to serving the public interest or at least behaved as if they were. After that they succumbed to the seductions created by the *infitah* (Open Door policy) and privatization. Some like to attribute this change to the presence of Nasser as president and then his absence, but I am inclined to explain it by citing the change in Egypt's social and economic conditions, as well as the change in the general international climate.

Egyptians began the decade of the 1950s poor and they ended the decade of the 1960s poor, but the revolution of 1952 offered them hope for better conditions. Many things gave them reasons for being confident that their situation and that of their children might really improve, including agricultural reform, income redistribution, the imposition of a minimum wage, free education, guaranteed employment for college graduates, and progressive taxation. All of this was properly implemented, and the resulting leveling between the classes was real, hence the widespread sense of equality among Egyptians. There was no offensively conspicuous consumption that might have rocked the boat enough to motivate people to seek extra money by any means.

Despite the increased rate of economic development between the mid-1950s and the mid-1960s, the rate of inflation remained low, and the income of the lower classes kept up with it as the real income for the overwhelming majority of them rose. Social mobility did rise after the revolution, but what kept the social mobility of the 1950s and 1960s from producing the level of social tension that it brought about in the 1970s and the 1980s was an inability or a reluctance to break the law. The desire to imitate the upper classes was less strong because of the absence (or at least the limited scope) of conspicuous consumption; the new regime's protectionist measures, which prohibited or severely limited the import of goods, the purchase of which was beyond the capacity of most Egyptians; and the limited spread of television, as well as the sedate and completely non-commercial nature of its programs.

Throughout the 1960s, the exchange value of the Egyptian pound declined to the point that bank employees outside Egypt looked at it askance, hardly knowing what it was. Why would non-Egyptians ask for Egyptian pounds from their banks? Egypt did not export anything of significance except for cotton, tourism was not important, and non-Egyptians were leaving Egypt faster than others were coming in. While it was completely forbidden for Egyptians to take Egyptian pounds out of the country, there was no demand worth mentioning for the pound outside of Egypt. But in Egypt the pound maintained its value through-out the 1950s and 1960s, for the inflation rate did not exceed 2 or 3 percent. Egyptian goods were produced almost solely for the Egyptian people, and almost all goods and services on offer were locally made and denominated in Egyptian pounds. It was later, during the 1970s, that Egypt began to split into two nations: one whose earnings and expenditures were in dollars (or at least whose goods and services were valued in dollars) and the other whose earnings and expenditures were in Egyptian pounds. One nation wore imported clothing, ate imported foods, furnished its houses with imported furniture, and spent its holidays abroad; the other wore Egyptian clothes and ate Egyptian food, and did not travel abroad except in search of employment. This necessarily sharpened the motivation to cross the divide between the two even, if necessary, by immoral or illegal means. Things were different in the 1950s and 1960s. Of course, the dollar had its allure, even then, but it did not have the magic it acquired later. What, in any case, could anybody do with it when importing dollars was so restricted and leaving the country with dollars was forbidden?

Beginning with the 1952 revolution and up until the military defeat of 1967, a powerful sense of belonging prevailed among Egyptians, along with the hope that the nation could revive itself and realize its dreams. The patriotic poems of Salah Jahin sung by 'Abd al-Halim Hafez[5] were not written by a madman or sung by a hypocrite; they reflected the true sentiments of the great majority of Egyptians at the time. In such a climate, acts of corruption and bribery were viewed with a mixture of contempt and astonishment. One cannot deny that such acts did occur, such as a high-ranking officer acquiring a choice chalet in the grounds of the Muntazah Gardens in Alexandria, or some upper-level manager changing more than the permitted amount of hard currency so that he might bring a pile of hard-to-get presents home with him from a trip abroad, but such violations were infrequent and customs regulations were generally strictly enforced. Likewise were building regulations, tax laws, and hiring and promotion regulations in both the government and the public sector.

The situation was not merely one of low motivation for breaking the law; the Egyptian state in the 1950s and 1960s was also capable of thwarting any attempt at lawbreaking. When, in the mid-1960s, a high government official said, "the law should be given a vacation," he did not mean allowing people to do as they pleased, but exactly the opposite: he meant that if any law existed that forbade the government from imposing its will on the people or protected them from its interference in their lives, then that law should be given a holiday.

The constant presence of authority was, indeed, an effective measure limiting the extent of corruption in Egypt in the 1950s and 1960s, but one must acknowledge that there are several types of corruption, and that the desire for illegal income and wealth is only one of them; the lust for pure power is another. The power of the Egyptian president, even as it had grown after the removal of Muhammad Naguib, the first president after the revolution, had not yet transformed itself into what could be called a police state as began to appear after a series of nationalizations, beginning with the nationalization of the Suez Canal in 1956 and continuing until the mid-1960s. Throughout that period, one after another of the founding members of the revolutionary council fell from power, leaving behind only the president and a very few 'yes' men. This absolute power was not used, as I have previously explained, for amassing wealth, except rarely and to the most limited extent, but it was certainly exploited, and at an increasing rate, to accumulate power and widen the sphere of influence. This is in effect a kind of corruption since it represents sacrificing the public good for private benefit.

The lust for power did indeed hurt the public good, and Egypt saw many examples of this in the 1960s. One of the most important of these was the choice of a head of the armed forces with no qualifications for the job except the president's confidence that he would not lead a revolt against him, or the president's appointment of a vice president—without consulting anyone—for reasons that must have had little to do with concern for public welfare. Once this vice president had become president, corruption of the money-hungry kind surpassed any that Egypt had witnessed in Nasser's era or under the monarchy. Thus, corruption opened a new and dismal page during the 1970s, or, to be precise, a little before the 1970s began, for the defeat of 1967 was not only a military, political, and economic disaster, it also had the added effect of weakening the incentives for Egyptians to elevate the common good over private gain.

4

How could an incident that lasted no more than five days have such an effect on the life of an entire nation, bringing the revolution to a halt, spreading despair among the people, and directing a severe blow to their sense of belonging to the country? The ruling regime was afflicted with weakness and inability to enforce the law. The rate of growth of the economy dropped to the point where it barely exceeded the rate of population growth. A high degree of irrationality crept into religious discourse, with credence given to all kinds of miracles and superstition. Ritual and outward appearance were elevated above moral commitment, and Muslims became increasingly prepared to abuse Copts without provocation, causing the Copts increased anxiety. In such a climate, is it any wonder that corruption would grow at an unprecedented rate? It was as if the heart failed and blood stopped being pumped to various parts of the body, which became subject to decomposition. It was as if the state, defeated in 1967, became so fearful of the rich that it was ready to overlook their caprices, and to permit them and others to smuggle banned goods into Egypt and large amounts of cash out.

Meanwhile, it became necessary to placate the middle class—whom the military defeat affected probably more than it did any other segment of society—by making available some of the goods it had coveted but was unable to acquire, and to allow it to enjoy some types of entertainment that had previously been unavailable. A few racy films and some luxury items found their way into the consumer co-ops; foreign publishers, usually subject to strict censorship, were permitted to display their books at the annual Cairo International Book Fair, which was established soon after 1967; and some plays critical of the regime were allowed to be staged as an outlet for venting people's anger.

It suddenly became possible for people with the means to do so to amass small fortunes by opening a restaurant or an amusement park while neglecting to pay the taxes imposed under the socialist laws. Regulations for university entrance were relaxed, such that secondary school graduates were admitted without much distinction being made between those who deserved a university education and those who did not. The important thing was to please the masses and prevent giving them some new cause to grumble. There also seemed no harm in using religion in the media for the good of the state to admonish people to a point of fatalistic endurance under adversity and to encourage adherence to the outward forms of worship, on the off-chance that they may stop thinking about their current circumstances. This was tied to and aided by an attempt to revive a sense of pride in Egyptian history as a means of solace for the calamities of the moment, and the promotion of aspects of cultural heritage, such as classical Arabic music, and of sports, in which people might find similar comfort.

There is no society in any era entirely lacking in people willing to engage in corruption, just as there will always be germs floating in the air; but some climates weaken the resistance to germs and some strengthen it. The climate that prevailed after the defeat of 1967 was of the type that weakens resistance and fosters contagion.

The sense of loyalty to the nation engendered by the revolution of 1952 and the series of successes it attained in domestic and foreign policies was bound to weaken as a result of the military defeat. Suffering such a disgrace, the regime lost most of its power to impose its will and enforce respect for the law. Some members of the educated elite emigrated, but a much more common reaction was for large numbers of people to begin to look to their own affairs instead of concerning themselves with national or public issues. Some politicians turned into investors, some talented composers became traders, and some university professors turned to lucrative private tutoring. But the chance for real self-enrichment did not really soar until after another eight years, that is, in the mid-1970s, when new opportunities for corruption emerged.

A new president had been installed five years previously when Sadat took power after Nasser's death in 1970. As I have noted earlier, Sadat's personality was very much suited to the new political and social climate. But even Sadat was incapable of committing outrageous acts of corruption while the climate was not conducive to it. Such acts as appropriating the mansion of an officer (simply because his wife liked it) did not happen until after Nasser appointed him vice president in 1969. Nasser contented himself with expressing his anger for a short while, and then gave him a mansion on the Nile as compensation. Before that, Sadat had limited his activities of this type to accepting lavish gifts. This change was to be observed in the behavior of other important personalities who played prominent roles in both eras.

With the onset of an era of hyperinflation following the 1973 war and the inauguration of the Open Door policy, a flood of conspicuous consumption goods poured into Egypt and the rate of labor migration to the Gulf countries increased dramatically, pushing up the rate of social mobility. Television responded to this new situation and people saw on the small screen new types of serials and programs expressing new ambitions. Television also began to rely upon revenues from advertising, with some of the advertisements becoming more popular than the programs themselves. All of this inflamed the fever of consumerism and a good section of Egyptians discovered for the first time the true meaning of 'the good life': the life of high consumption and luxury.

Thus did Egypt during the second half of the Sadat era witness hitherto unknown examples of corruption in various fields. In schools and universities the phenomenon of trade in textbooks, whereby teachers require their students to buy books of their authorship, became widespread, and private lessons became common. The basis for choosing university presidents and deans changed: it was no longer based upon the candidate's scholarly standing or reputation (as it had been up until the end of the 1950s), or his readiness to promote the slogans of socialism (as it was in the 1960s), instead it was based on the candidate's readiness to avert his eyes from infractions of the law on campus. Now, the same faculty members who had written books extolling socialism set about compiling new books defending the *infitah*. With the launch of the *infitah*, nepotism and patronage spread through the economy, and the state began building projects of doubtful value other than serving the interests of those who had the ear of those in power. The commissions garnered by the government elites increased beyond limit, while huge incentives began to appear for the directors of public sector companies willing to enter into joint ventures with foreign companies. Encroachment on agricultural lands for the building of illegal residential units increased to the extent that what was lost in agricultural area under Sadat was nearly equal to what had been gained from the High Dam.

Soon after President Sadat's assassination, people discovered the size of the fortune Esmat al-Sadat had amassed during his brother's term in office. Not only did the extent of corruption become clear, but also the extent of consumption fever and the insatiable appetite for wealth. It turned out that what Sadat's brother had amassed during his brother's reign included not only agricultural and residential real estate, villas, and apartment buildings, but also shops, factories, warehouses, workshops, civilian and commercial means of transport, import–export agencies, and contracting companies, all extending from the farthest north of the country to the farthest south.

The growth of corruption during the 1970s was closely associated with a large increase in state revenues and a high rate of economic growth, along with the flood of remittances from abroad to the families of expatriate workers. This boom in revenues permitted an increase in opportunities for illegal practices, but it also diminished the public's appetite for stamping out corruption. It seemed that everyone, including large numbers of the agricultural population, was sharing in a grand festival mingling the honest with the criminal, with both elements trumpeting their brilliant successes in class mobility.

In such a climate, both the form and content of religious discourse were bound to change, incorporating language and rituals that concealed what was happening and covered with a veil of piety something that was its exact opposite. One famous deliverer of such discourse was to declare in his televised speeches that great wealth was a sign of God's pleasure, without uttering a word condemning the prevalent order of corruption. Despite their lax attitude toward corruption, the enormous popularity of such spokesmen for religion was not diminished. Indeed, a prop for their position came from the president himself in his frequent use of religious slogans and his constant extolling of what he called the "values of the village," whatever that was supposed to mean. It was as if he in turn was using this type of discourse to cover up the increasing corruption of his regime.

The death of Sadat did not put an end to all of this; it just took on different forms beginning in the 1980s. While corruption under Nasser was greatly limited in scope and denounced firmly whenever it was discovered, it turned into a large jamboree under Sadat, with everyone participating joyfully and fearlessly seizing any opportunity presented to them. During the Mubarak era, the denunciations became much weaker and the joy vanished, as if corruption had become institutionalized. Little by little throughout the 1980s, corruption became routine and was no longer thought shameful. This needs some elaboration.

5

A totalitarian government encourages corruption by its continuous interference in every large and small aspect of life; the soft state encourages corruption by its very softness. What should one expect from a state that is both totalitarian and soft? This is how the Egyptian state has appeared since the 1980s. Even if it is not as totalitarian as the Nasserist state, it has retained many of the restrictions on individual freedoms imposed by the Nasser administration. Sadat abolished the depredations of the police state and did away with what were called 'visitors of the wee hours.' So, too, did he cancel many restrictions on imports; but the freeing of the economy remained otherwise limited until the end of his term. The Mubarak administration inherited a large public sector, even if it had become greatly weakened and worn out by the state's withdrawal of protection, thereby exposing it to severe competition from imports. Sadat had, in 1971, already abolished so-called 'centers of power,' which had severely limited political and individual freedoms; but the venerable Egyptian bureaucracy, which reached its apogee under Nasser, remained exceedingly cumbersome under both Sadat and Mubarak, and, thus, the impetus to engage in corruption remained in place simply for getting round bureaucratic restrictions. Under Mubarak, however, the state grew increasingly incapable, even more so than under Sadat, of curbing corruption. Was this weakness simply the result of a change in the character of the ruler? That might have had some effect, but it was certainly not the major factor. The main causes seem to have something to do with the change that came over national ambitions, and the change in Egypt's relationship with foreign powers.

The national ambition in the pre-revolutionary era was as simple and clear as it could be: to bring the British occupation to an end. At the time, Egyptian political parties differed among themselves in their approach to realizing this goal; the Wafd and the National Party were the most fervent in this, but other parties as well as the independents, whenever they gained some power, could not help but devote all of their energies to working toward the same goal, even if by way of diplomacy and negotiations.

After the British withdrew in 1956, Nasser used new slogans for the people to rally around and formulated what, in the eyes of the great majority, became a new 'national project.' It revolved around the liberation of the Egyptian economy from foreign domination, rapid economic development, the reduction of class disparities, and extending support for Arab movements outside of Egypt in combating colonialism and particularly in supporting the Palestinian struggle against Zionism.

In the Sadat era, all this came to an end: the struggle for complete British withdrawal had ended, the struggle to free the Egyptian economy of foreign domination and the nationalization of Egyptian industry were abandoned, and so was the support for other Arab movements of liberation from colonialism and Zionism. The 'national project' under Sadat was reduced to the liberation of Egyptian land that Israel had occupied in 1967; this goal took up the entire Sadat era, and was not achieved until Sadat's signing of the peace agreement in 1979, that is, only shortly before he was assassinated. Indeed, perhaps his signing of the peace agreement was itself the cause of his assassination.

By the time Mubarak came to power, none of these ambitions remained. He had nothing left before him by way of freeing Egypt from colonialism, freeing the economy, or supporting Arab nationalist movements. The issue of Israeli occupation of Egyptian land was about to be resolved with the Israeli withdrawal from the last bit of Sinai, namely the withdrawal from the port city of Taba on the Egyptian–Israeli border which was being negotiated and was completed in 1982. What, then, was Mubarak to struggle for? He had begun his term with the release of political prisoners incarcerated by Sadat in 1981 and the return of press freedom to the opposition newspapers. Then what? He had nothing of consequence to promise to the Egyptians, no clear project to drive him forward.

This is not to say, of course, that with the coming of Mubarak there was nothing left for the Egyptians to set their hearts on. There was, for example, the task of correcting the numerous errors committed by Sadat with regard to economic and foreign policy. He might have tried to put an end to the neglect that the agricultural sector had suffered throughout the 1970s; or to steer the Open Door policy toward faster industrialization instead of exposing Egyptian industry to crippling competition from imports; or to protect the poorer sections of the population from the ruinous effects of runaway inflation. He might have worked to effect true democracy by putting an end to the falsification of election results; or to correct Sadat's policy toward other Arab states and try to return to Egypt her lost place in the Arab world, using what remained within her grasp to compel Israel to grant concessions to the Palestinians; or to try to take a more independent stand vis-à-vis the United States.

Indeed, Egyptians' hopes along these lines were raised in the first few months of Mubarak's rule; those hopes soon evaporated when it became clear that he had no intention of doing anything of the sort, and that the mistakes that Sadat had initiated would persist throughout the Mubarak era. Indeed, President Mubarak's personality was well-suited to continuing along the path that Sadat had set without any deviation, but one should also acknowledge that the personality of the president cannot be decisive in determining Egyptian development. Rather, the defining factor was Egypt's relation with foreign powers, and that was essentially determined by the changes in international relations.

President Sadat had placed Egypt in the orbit of the United States in 1972 when he ousted the Soviets from Egypt. From the mid-1970s onward the situation did not look very different from Egypt's submission to Britain before the 1952 revolution, but there was one important difference between the two situations with regard to the issue with which we are concerned: corruption.

The British interest in Egypt during the first half of the twentieth century was indeed very simple when compared to that of the Americans in the second half. At the end of the day, British interests revolved around buying cheap Egyptian cotton, opening the local market to British goods such as textiles, and acquiring a strategic position on the Suez Canal. All of these goals could be accomplished within a reasonable amount of respect for the law and a high degree of integrity in the Egyptian administration. Compare that with major American interests in Egypt since the early 1970s: opening the Egyptian market for a great variety of goods from weapons to soft drinks; the privatization of one company after another and one bank after another in the interest of American or multinational firms; forcing Egypt to comply with Israeli interests in Egypt and the Arab world; and using American economic and military aid to enforce continued submission to and the realization of such goals. All of this required a very different political regime from that which prevailed before the revolution, or under Nasser, and even different from that which prevailed under Sadat. Such a regime was indeed of a kind most conducive to an increase in corruption.

6

The first prime minister of the Mubarak era was the last prime minister in the whole era to have had some knowledge of political history, or to have even possessed a real interest in politics. After him came prime ministers without any political background to speak of. Indeed, before assuming their positions, many of them were known for eschewing politics in favor of their private interests or their narrow business concerns. What kind of ministers would such men bring along with them, other than those who are mainly concerned with their own private interests?

During the past twenty years a number of powerful elements have thus gathered together to produce a degree of corruption among various sections of Egyptian society the like of which had not been seen in the 1950s, 1960s, or 1970s, nor even in pre-revolutionary Egypt. There was now a weak state that lost both the power and the will to punish those transgressing the law, with no commitment to a national project which could unite the people, but which attached the greatest importance to currying favor with a certain foreign power that protects it and grants it aid. Meanwhile, the Egyptian people have become exposed to previously unknown levels of consumption prevailing outside the country so that they have gradually come to consider the possession of certain goods and the accumulation of wealth as the only measures of success. Respect for learning and academic credentials has declined, and the prestige of being a minister in the cabinet has eroded to the extent that few care to recall a minister's name. External pressure on the state to sell one public company after another to foreign buyers at less than their true value has become increasingly apparent, while state-owned lands have been sold at bargain prices to influential people who would build lofty villas on them or, as soon as the price doubles, resell them at the new price.

The state continues, however, to own newspapers, magazines, and the largest publishing house in Egypt, periodically announcing the names of new editors-in-chief. The state also decides who is or is not accepted into university, and who does or does not appear on television, and even provides financial assistance to opposition political parties so that it can maintain the appearance of democracy. In such a totalitarian but weak state how can corruption fail to spread like forest fire? A close bond has been formed between wealth and political decision-makers such that it was not regarded as odd that at least six government ministers might be appointed in a single government, each of whom was put in charge of a ministry closely related to the field of his commercial dealings prior to and after his government post, thus, as the old saying goes, "putting the fox in charge of the henhouse." This was just the sort of thing that would have caused a huge uproar in the pre-revolutionary era—if ever one were thought to be mixing public and private interest in this manner.

Huge loans were handed out without collateral by state banks to people close to the seats of power, who then fled the country without paying them off. A chief editor of a government-owned newspaper could amass a huge fortune by siphoning off advertisement revenues that ought to be accruing to the state, in exchange for personal and political favors provided to men in power, and then refuse to leave his post upon reaching retirement age, with the government doing nothing to dislodge him. Bogus companies were established for putatively religious purposes, collecting the savings of small shareholders and investing them in doubtful or illegal concerns right under the nose of the government in exchange for sky-high dividends to high-ranking officials, all charged off in what was called the 'Blessings Account,' and so on.

While this has been going on in the upper levels of society, other factors have been working to spread corruption among the middle and lower levels. The rapid rate of population growth, combined with insufficient economic growth and the slackening of labor migration, plus the resulting rise in unemployment and the growth of slums were all powerful enough motivators for people to circumvent the law.

Social mobility also slowed down from the mid-1980s onward, after rising in the previous decade, thus providing its own incentive to corruption. The reduced migration rate to the oil-producing countries of the Gulf and the return of a large number of migrants to Egypt ruined many people's hopes for greater social status. Inflation remained high throughout the 1980s and rose further at the end of the 1990s, dealing a huge blow to wide segments of the middle class and causing them to fear for their status. This created fertile ground for law-breaking, while the political changes at the highest levels severely weakened the patriotic sentiments of these segments of the middle class as they became ever more immersed in the problems of day-to-day life.

As examples of violations of the law increased and people heard of one example of corruption after another in various spheres of life, they grew accustomed to it and stopped expecting anything different. The more people got used to it, the more the rich and powerful found it easy to engage in it, and it has become common to hear excuses like, "corruption exists in every country in the world, so what exactly are you complaining about?" Bribes, large and small, have come to be widely expected, and are paid and received in the open without any embarrassment; more and more employees have come to consider them as part of their monthly salaries. On the other hand, those who are obliged to pay bribes have come to regard them as requisite fees. They are considered as part of one's living expenses, much like the cost of goods and ordinary services. Add the government's insouciance toward any complaints of corruption, the rarity of any complaints reaching the courts, and the disdain with which those in power hold any court injunction that may be handed down if an infraction actually reaches the court—and you have what is called 'the institutionalization of corruption': corruption has itself become the law that cannot be broken.

3

The Economy

1

In judging the economic performance of a country like Egypt, three standard indicators are usually used to assess its success or failure. What has happened to per capita income, that is, the rate of growth in total output minus the rate of population growth? What are the major components of this income (or national output)? Or, in other words, what is the relative contribution to total output coming from agriculture, manufacturing, petroleum products, tourism, and services? (This is what we usually refer to as economic structure.) What has happened to income distribution among various segments of society? Is it becoming more or less equal? These, then, are the three standard measures we use to gauge the quality of economic performance: the growth rate of Gross Domestic (or National) Product, structural change, and change in income distribution.

This makes a lot of sense: the ultimate aim of economic activity is to increase economic welfare (that is, welfare arising from the consumption of goods and services). Economic welfare depends in turn on the increase in the amount of goods and services produced compared to the rate of increase in population, how much more or less equitable is their distribution, and upon the nature of the goods and services produced, that is, the sector producing them—are they predominantly agricultural, industrial, or other kinds of goods and services? On the one hand, success in developing some sectors, like agriculture or mining, might contribute little to development in succeeding periods, while excessive reliance upon some other sectors, like tourism or remittances from workers abroad, may threaten growth with severe fluctuations from one period to the next. On the other hand, the rapid growth of some sectors, such as manufacturing, is seen to promise a more durable development in the future than would continued reliance upon agriculture, mining, tourism, or other services. The ultimate goal of economic policy for a country at Egypt's stage of development, then, is to guarantee (by means of changing the economic structure) a sustainable rise in material prosperity (growth) for the greatest number of people possible (distribution).

The position of Egyptian economists on the adoption of these standard indicators for determining and defining economic goals has not undergone significant change over time. Thus, successive governments continue to announce their successes with reference to these three indicators, and the opposition continues to announce the government's failures and to cast blame based upon one or more of these same three indicators. Let us, then, assess the economic changes that have occurred over the 1948–2008 period using these three criteria. I have chosen the period of sixty years as a frame to include part of the pre-revolution era as well.

It is interesting to note that economic issues did not have the same prominence among Egyptian concerns during the monarchical period that they do today. It was believed, quite correctly, that economic problems could not be solved in a manner satisfactory to national aspirations without Egyptians first reclaiming their country from the British. The British had imposed economic policies that were not conducive to the realization of the three goals just mentioned. They did not encourage industrialization and, as a result, the rate of growth remained dependent on the performance of agriculture. But Egyptian agriculture has a very limited capacity to raise income because of the small amount of arable land relative to the population. It was also obviously in the interests of the British that income distribution should remain as inequitable as it was, as the feudal landholders' interests were tied to those of the British.

This does not mean that concern was not expressed about the three economic issues: economic growth, income redistribution, and industrialization, but it is interesting to note that slogans revolving around the concepts of 'growth' and 'development' had not yet emerged to any significant degree in Egypt, nor, indeed, elsewhere. The goal of increasing national income or output, even if it now appears to us to be so obvious, was only mentioned occasionally before 1952. The most obvious explanation is that concern about raising national income had to await the introduction of national income accounting. The very concept of national income and the means of measuring it were not yet common, even in the more developed countries, before the 1940s. The first fruits of the nascent interest in national income accounting in Egypt came with the publication of the doctoral dissertation of Mahmoud Anis in the early 1940s. But there was another reason for the emergence of a strong interest in the issue of economic development after the end of the Second World War. The end of the war inaugurated what may be called 'the American Era,' which followed the old colonial rule by the British and the French. Starting from the mid-1940s, the United States came gradually to inherit the legacy of the two old colonial powers, but the new superpower was keen on announcing that its goal in the countries that gained their independence was to help them to achieve rapid 'economic development.' This was the term that the American president Truman used, as if by doing so he was ushering in a new era. Since that time, economists, universities, and United Nations organizations have all been preoccupied with the concept of 'economic growth and development.'

What I find very interesting is how the style of expressing economic goals changed between the monarchical era (when Egypt was under British rule) and the 1950s, following the 1952 revolution. Before 1952, Egyptian economists and policy-makers would usually express their main economic goals for Egypt as the eradication of three things: poverty, illiteracy, and disease. It is important to note, however, that what was generally meant by 'poverty' (now understood to mean a low per capita income) was a low income for a certain and less privileged part of the Egyptian population, particularly the rural population. Likewise, the words 'illiteracy' and 'disease' referred to the state of a particular section and not to the whole of the population or a fictitious average person. What was meant by problems of health in Egypt at that time was not the low number of doctors or hospitals per one thousand people, as is often meant now, but rather the incidence of certain specific diseases like bilharzia, especially among the rural population, arising from the lack of potable water, as well as other illnesses resulting from malnutrition.

The conception of economic goals at that time is significant because it reveals a simple, clear, and direct formulation and diagnosis of economic problems, as opposed to today's roundabout way, which is bound to distract attention from the real problems and could lead to mistaken policies in dealing with them. To speak about poverty by referring to real flesh-and-blood poor people, whose professions and places of residence are known, is different from expressing poverty by an arithmetic average referring to the state of the entire nation, encompassing the rich as well as the poor. Mistaken anti-poverty policies may therefore be implemented that end up making the rich richer and the poor poorer.

There was also much talk before the fall of the monarchy of the problem of income distribution, when disparities between the incomes and lifestyles of the rich and poor were too evident to be missed by anyone. The population had doubled during the first half of the twentieth century from ten to twenty million, while the amount of cultivated agricultural land had not increased by more than a quarter, from four million feddans to five million. Under a social system that permitted landowners to expand their holdings without limit, and with the very slow increase in investment opportunities outside of agriculture, land prices and rents continued to soar, while the wage for agricultural labor remained close to subsistence level. Tenant farmers were squeezed between the fixed agricultural wages, which were already as low as they could go, and the constantly increasing rents taken from them by landowners, owing to the growing scarcity of agricultural land compared to the demand for it.

There were, then, three possible solutions to the problem of income distribution: placing an upper limit on agricultural landholdings and redistributing the remaining land among the landless poor (what is known as agricultural reform); levying high taxes on the rent paid to landowners and using the tax revenue to the benefit of those of limited income; or making a concerted effort to accelerate the process of industrialization, which would create new job opportunities outside of agriculture. The political system prevailing before the revolution stood in the way of all of these three solutions: most of the members of the political elite (including members of parliament) were themselves feudal landlords and could obstruct the passing of any law effecting agricultural reform or greatly increasing the tax burden on land holdings. Meanwhile, the British allowed only limited industrialization.

While Egypt was certainly poor compared to Europe and North America, she was richer than all other Arab states, except the small state of Lebanon, and more advanced than all of them in education, also with the exception of Lebanon as well as Palestine. Oil had indeed been discovered in the Gulf states, but oil revenues were still quite limited and were not enough to allow the oil-producing states to change their long-held view of Egypt as the political heavyweight of the region and the most socially advanced Arab nation with the finest university and cultural production in the Arab world. Indeed, Egypt continued to produce and send to Saudi Arabia annually the cloth mantle (the *kiswa*) for the Ka'ba, the holiest shrine of Islam, and to send pens and notebooks as gifts to schools in Kuwait. Egypt had also advanced further than either China or India in terms of industrialization and income level and was not on both counts too far behind Turkey, where the Atatürk revolution had resulted in greater economic progress than that achieved by Egypt during the interwar period. But Egypt, being the host to al-Azhar University, the seat of Sunni Islamic learning, attracted students from all over the Arab and Muslim worlds, who were granted scholarships by the Egyptian government to cover their living expenses while studying in Egypt.

Even though Egypt had been defeated by Israel only four years before the 1952 revolution, in the Palestine war in 1948, Israel remained for several years after 1948 not much ahead of Egypt in terms of average income or in level of industrialization, and not even in terms of military capability. Egypt was indeed a poor nation at the advent of the July Revolution of 1952, but was viewed both by Egyptians and the rest of the world as holding great promise for development, possessing the necessary human and natural resources. The revolution further raised those hopes. So what exactly happened to squander such high hopes?

2

It is quite appropriate to name the period from 1952 to 1967 the Nasserist Era, even though Nasser was not president for the first two years after the revolution, and remained president until the end of his life in 1970. This is because Nasser's influence was dominant even under the first president, Muhammad Naguib, and declined immensely after the defeat of 1967.

When the famous Six Principles of the revolution were announced in 1952, economic progress did not occupy an important position among them. This was an expression of the prevailing climate in Egypt at the time and was not inconsistent with the political sphere outside of Egypt, too. The emphasis of the day was on gaining independence and ending colonialism more than it was on development. It is true that one of the most important of all economic and social laws passed by the regime in its entire existence, namely the Land Reform Law, was passed in September 1952 only two months after the revolution. But the main goal of this law was political rather than economic. One aim was indeed the redistribution of ownership and income in the agricultural sector in favor of the landless and poor farmers, and another was to redirect the savings of the middle class from the purchase of agricultural lands to investment in industry. But its main goal, and it was more successful in this than in achieving the others, was to trim the claws of the large landholders and put an end to their political and social influence.

Serious steps toward increasing the pace of economic development, the rate of industrialization, and the redistribution of income outside of the agricultural sector did not begin until the second half of the 1950s, and did not continue for much longer than ten years. Thus, everything that characterizes the Nasserist era, at least in the economic sphere, took place during the short period from 1956 to 1967. This period began with the nationalization of the Suez Canal, followed by the launching of an ambitious industrial program in 1958, and then by an even more ambitious five-year plan for the period 1960 to 1965, which was successful beyond all expectations. This was followed by sweeping nationalization of industrial and commercial firms, banks, and insurance companies, including some large retail firms. Then came the military defeat of 1967, putting a decisive end to all of this.

It was a brilliant success gauged by all three standard indicators. The rate of growth of national output in the period 1956 to 1967 reached 6 percent and, with a rate of population growth of 2.8 percent, per capita income increased by 3.2 percent annually. This was regarded, at least by the standards of the time, as a very good performance, especially in view of the virtual stagnation of per capita income during the previous half century and in light of the relatively high rate of population growth compared to what it is at present. It is not true, then, as is often said now, that public ownership harmed economic development in Egypt, or that agricultural reform lowered agricultural productivity. The source of all such accusations is, rather, the trend that has prevailed since the 1970s in development literature and has been propagated by international organizations, which mounted a relentless attack on public ownership and rejected advocacy of a large role for government in the economy.

What is also notable is how such a good economic performance was realized during the period between 1956 and 1967 while the middle class was being pampered compared to how it was treated under other socialist regimes, and without creating an unbearable burden of foreign debt. Of course, imports were subject to severe restrictions during this period as were transfers of funds out of the country, harsh conditions were imposed on private investment, and tax rates were raised significantly. Despite that, any fair assessment of the state of the Egyptian middle class at the time must conclude that this segment of the population was treated quite mildly considering the ambitious goals set for economic development and in view of the very low level of income of most Egyptians. The inflation rate remained quite low throughout the 1950s and 1960s, despite the magnitude of development efforts, and complaints about rising prices were rarely heard. Appropriate housing continued to be available at moderate rents thanks to rent control laws. People of all classes were not lacking in any of the necessities of life, even if they were of lower quality compared with what had previously been imported. The larger part of the middle class accepted such restrictions; the high degree of justice in their implementation and the equality with which they were applied lessened the sense of deprivation. Indeed, the development plan permitted the production of goods like automobiles, air conditioners, and refrigerators at prices within easy reach of a large section of the middle class.

What was it that allowed Egypt to achieve this high level of economic performance during the period between 1956 and 1967? I do not think it necessary to exaggerate the wisdom or good behavior of those in power at the time. To be sure, one must admit to their sincerity and to the high degree of integrity among them. No doubt they were encouraged in this by the popular support given them, which spurred them on to try to maintain this popularity. Admittedly there were examples to the contrary, but the general picture of work in the economic realm during that time was worthy of admiration. Nevertheless, one must acknowledge that the main factor behind the positive economic performance of the period was the prevailing international climate and not any domestic factor. I have already said that what can be called the true Nasserist era, at least in the economic arena, started with the nationalization of the Suez Canal in 1956, which brought Egypt significant revenue that had previously been going to the Suez Canal Company and overnight made Nasser into a hero, not just of Egypt, but of all the Arabs, and one of the noteworthy leaders of the Third World. Earning this new status enabled Nasser to take other economic measures, such as the nationalization of foreign banks and major foreign companies, or to Egyptianize them, immediately after the nationalization of the Suez Canal. In 1958 he put in place an industrialization program and the first five-year plan in the following year. After that came the nationalization of Egyptian companies in 1961, and in that same year he took revolutionary measures to redistribute income. The successful nationalization of the Suez Canal and the forced withdrawal of Israeli, French, and British forces, after their attack on Egypt and Israel's occupation of Sinai in reaction to the nationalization, would never have happened without the Americans' and Soviets' united stand behind Nasser and their endorsement of the nationalization of the Canal, even though the United States would occasionally show signs of opposing it. The American goal was obviously to eliminate British and French influence in the region, and the nationalization of the Canal and the emergence of a strong leader, all in the name of ending colonialism, seem to have suited very well the achievement of this goal. For their part, the Soviets saw no harm in supporting this new leader as long as he did not fall into the arms of the Americans. The period between 1956 and 1967 was the era of 'non-alignment' and 'positive neutrality,' and the emergence of the Third World as a new power, and it was, for the same reasons, the golden age of foreign aid that poured from east and west into some selected Third World countries, with Egypt being one of the biggest aid recipients.

Could Egypt have built the High Dam in Aswan, financed its ambitious industrialization program, or embarked on an even more ambitious five-year plan without this stream of Soviet and American aid? While the Soviets funded the High Dam and the new factories, the Americans provided Egypt with wheat and other food aid, both on very concessionary terms: long-term repayment periods at very low interest rates and, in the case of American aid, payable in Egyptian pounds. Strong evidence for the importance of this flow of funds from abroad was that once American aid stopped altogether in 1967, to be replaced by open enmity from the United States and a surprisingly passive attitude from the Soviet Union, the rate of growth in Egypt fell sharply in the following eight years.

The success of Nasser's economic policies cannot be denied; the rates of growth of total and per capita income rose significantly as well as the share of manufacturing in total output and in exports, and income distribution became much more equitable than it had been at the time of the revolution. There is no doubt that Nasser's personality, his intelligence, and his strong sense of patriotism played an important part in all this, but a lot of credit must also go to favorable international circumstances. As soon as those circumstances changed, Nasser lost most of his magic and his leadership of Egypt, the Arabs, and the rest of the Third World was greatly weakened.

3

Sadat inherited from Nasser an economy bearing many strong features built during the golden era of 1956 to 1967, but he also inherited a military defeat that imposed a heavy burden on the economy. More importantly, he came into an international climate utterly hostile to any attempt to repeat the Nasserist experience. Foreign aid was reduced severely as an outcome of the new rapprochement reached between the Soviets and the Americans, as was the aid coming from international organizations. The Americans placed four strict conditions on Egypt for aid to be resumed: making peace with Israel, stepping down as the leader of Arab nationalism, opening the door to foreign goods and investment, and getting rid of Soviet influence. And the Soviets did not seem to oppose any of these conditions.

Sadat was not the type of man to try to oppose the demands made of him in this new international climate; instead, he was a 'realist,' that is, he was ready to adjust to whatever reality he faced, whereas Nasser was by his very temperament prone to challenge it. Sadat did all that was asked of him politically and economically. He launched the economic Open Door policy, or *infitah*, in 1974, without much regard to protecting Egyptian industry or maintaining a high rate of growth in the agricultural sector. He allowed imports to compete with locally produced goods and failed to provide the necessary public investment for growth in those two sectors. With the increase in remittances pouring in from migrant workers in the oil-producing countries, and with the return of Suez Canal revenues following its reopening in 1975, the restoration of oil fields in Sinai, the rise in oil prices, the resumption of foreign aid, as well as the revival of tourism, Egypt began to look as if it was going through a phase of unprecedented prosperity. Income and consumption rose sharply with a flood of imported consumer goods. Sadat and his supporters considered this a sign of economic revival resulting from his economic reforms, following two decades of deprivation. The rate of growth in national income reached more than 8 percent per annum between 1975 and 1985, causing an increase of more than 5 percent in per capita income, something Egypt had not seen in at least one hundred years. This prosperity was, however, like a beautiful mansion built on sand: the rate of growth in the manufacturing and agricultural sectors fell sharply because of the drop in public investment in both sectors, the neglect of maintenance and renovation of the public sector, and the decline in protection given to it from competing imports. The high rate of growth originated in unreliable and unsustainable sources. Remittances from abroad were dependent upon oil prices and on the policies of the Arab countries employing Egyptian workers. Oil prices fluctuate with international demand and the same is true of revenues from the Suez Canal and tourism, while foreign aid was, of course, governed by political considerations. The frailty of all these sources of income was confirmed in the mid-1980s.

In addition, Sadat followed a policy of excessive borrowing from abroad. At the time, western banks were seeking outlets to invest surplus oil revenues and began to flood Third World countries with loans at exorbitant interest rates, whether or not these countries actually needed them. Egypt certainly did not need such loans. Taking on loans of such magnitude in an era of prosperity had no justification. To make matters worse, a large part of these loans consisted of military loans at very high interest rates, at a time when Sadat was boasting that the October War of 1973 was to be Egypt's last war.

The growing burden of these loans on the Egyptian economy began to catch Sadat's attention only five years into his rule. In 1975 he declared that the debt situation was perilous, describing the Egyptian economy as having "reached the zero point," but offered strange justifications for this state of affairs, one of them being that no one had warned him beforehand how serious the situation was and that he had previously assumed that the amounts being presented to him were in dollars when it turned out that they were in pounds sterling. In 1975 alone, Egypt paid $2,083 million in principal repayment and interest on her short-term debt, which constituted about one third of the total Egyptian external debt. Interest rates on this short-term debt exceeded 15 percent, and the total 1975 payments in servicing Egypt's external debt equaled as much as 78 percent of the total export revenues for that year.

During this and the following year President Sadat made several visits, together with his prime minister and his ministers of finance and the economy, to the Gulf states to plead for an increase in the amount of Arab aid to Egypt. He used every argument he could muster, from the heroism of the Egyptian army in the October War and the sacrifices made by Egypt in the Palestinian cause to Egyptian contributions to the development of the Arab Gulf states, all to no avail. The answer of the oil states' governments at the time was that they were, in fact, giving all they could and that even if they could give more there was no guarantee that Egypt would put the extra aid to good use. There was also a hint at the waste and corruption of the Egyptian government, an excuse that must have sounded strange coming from these states, which were well known for squandering a good amount of their resources. They must have learned from officials of the World Bank and other international organizations that granting aid for debt payments encourages waste; that it was better to give direct aid to particular projects, rather than as general economic support, and that, unfortunately, Egypt did not have sufficient feasibility studies for these. The truth of the matter was that the Gulf governments had not yet obtained the go-ahead from the United States and international aid organizations to increase the amount of aid to Egypt, and that would not happen unless Egypt finally showed itself ready to accept the directives of the International Monetary Fund (IMF) and to take firm steps toward concluding a peace agreement with Israel. That was what happened when Sadat made his visit to Jerusalem in 1977 and signed a peace agreement with Israel in 1979.

Sadat's Open Door policy and reduced government intervention in the economy were sure to propel the economy in the opposite direction from that which it had taken under Nasser. As far as the issue of income distribution was concerned, the Open Door policy increased the opportunities for wealth enhancement for the upper strata while raising prices faster than wage increases. At the same time, the government reduced tax burdens on the rich while it lowered its spending on the poor, slowed the process of job creation for new graduates, a process that had started under Nasser, and reduced the rate of public investment, leading to slower job creation all round. The employment situation was saved only by the large increase in migration of Egyptian workers to the oil states. This opened up many new job opportunities for both educated and uneducated Egyptians while raising the standard of living for many of those remaining behind in Egypt. If migration contributed to an increased inflation rate, as a result of the inflow of remittances of migrant workers coming into Egypt, it also contributed to the creation of new sources of income for many Egyptians of limited means.

Migration dispelled a great many worries for Egyptians, boosting the income of many poor families even if it did nothing to reduce the gap between them and the nouveaux riches of the *infitah*. The part of society that was especially harmed by the *infitah*, and which saw its standard of living lowered, was the large segment of the middle class that had neither migrated nor found the means for increasing their income by working in the new *infitah* activities, such as import/export, brokerage, exchanging currencies, or renting out furnished apartments, and so on. This significant portion of the population, including most government employees, was hit hard by the *infitah* and by inflation, but its voice and grievances went unheard amid the hubbub of the *infitah* and migration.

In those days Sadat pinned great hopes on the inflow of private foreign investment to Egypt after he passed a law granting prospective investors many incentives and tax exemptions. So, too, did he hope that the local private sector would respond to the easing of government intervention in the economy by increasing private investment in industry and agriculture. But those hopes were dashed from two sides. Despite everything the government did to entice foreign investors, they did not respond. Private foreign investment does not come simply in response to economic incentives; an appropriate political climate must prevail as well. Such a climate includes things such as Egypt improving relations with Israel and the level of political stability. As for Egyptian investors, they would not put their money into industry and agriculture just because they found such investment profitable; they would have to see it as being more profitable than placing their money elsewhere. If they found it more profitable to invest in the import/export trade (but especially import trade), the building of luxury apartments, or in contracting and other types of services that flourished under the *infitah*, then they would, of course, prefer investing in them. This is one important reason that industry and agriculture suffered during the Sadat era. Thus, the economic structure changed noticeably, not for the betterment of industry and agriculture, but in favor of the service sector, especially commerce and construction. All of this was closely tied to the big increase in foreign debt, which would encumber future economic performance and ultimately reduce the rate of growth.

On Sadat's death in 1981, Egypt's external debt exceeded $30 billion, compared to $5 billion at the death of Nasser. That meant that Egypt's external debt of all types (military and civilian, private and public, and short-, medium-, and long-term) increased under Sadat by about sixfold. The result was not only a larger external debt in absolute terms than the notorious debt of Khedive Ismail a hundred years before ($30 billion compared to £91 million), but a far greater burden, be it in terms of percentage of national income or in terms of the ratio of debt service to Egyptian foreign exchange revenues.

4

The psychological makeup of President Hosni Mubarak would not permit him to change the direction of Egyptian economic policy that Sadat had taken; nor have his advisors, because of their own personalities and temperaments, found it in their own interests to advise him to change it. More important is that many of those advisors had been picked by Sadat at the beginning of his rule from among those owing allegiance to the United States, in the belief that the United States was the sole power capable of keeping him in office. Moreover, Sadat's signing of the peace agreement with Israel in 1979 caused the Arab states to cease granting aid to Egypt for many years as punishment for this unseemly behavior. Such circumstances pushed Egypt ever deeper into the American orbit and into greater reliance upon American aid.

Thus, President Mubarak continued to borrow from abroad for as long as such loans were available, only ceasing when the creditors had sucked the last drop of blood from the Egyptian economy and they, themselves, had no desire to continue. Not only did the patient's condition show no good prognosis for repayment, but they no longer had much money to lend after the big decline in surplus oil revenues.

During the first five years of the Mubarak era, Egypt's external debt continued to grow until the total military and civilian external debt reached $45 billion. That is, it rose by 50 percent over five years, which was still a lower rate of increase than that of the Sadat era. This continued until 1990, when the Gulf crisis erupted with Saddam Hussein's attack on Kuwait. In that year the total debt had reached $47.6 million, that is, 150 percent of the gross domestic product, making Egypt's debt burden one of the highest in the world as measured against domestic output, and higher than the already heavy debt burden Egypt had carried one hundred years previously (about 100 percent of GDP), which had led to the deposing of the ruler of the time (Khedive Ismail) and the British occupation.

In 1990, when the amount of Egypt's debt service had risen to $6 billion a year (representing 53 percent of the value of all Egypt's exports of goods and services), and the opportunities for commercial or government borrowing narrowed sharply, the nation began to face severe difficulty in paying for food imports. This was exactly the opportune moment for Shylock to demand his pound of flesh, which came in the form of Egypt's stance on the side of the United States against Saddam Hussein, to the extent of Egypt dispatching troops to fight alongside the Americans in return for waiving part of the debt that it had no way of repaying. It's interesting to note that in the six months following the start of the Gulf crisis, Egypt obtained promises of $4,726 million from several Arab countries, the most important of which were Saudi Arabia, Kuwait, and the United Arab Emirates; the same countries that had severed ties with Egypt and turned their backs on it only ten years before, allegedly because of the peace agreement with Israel. But more significant was the large amount of debt forgiveness that Egypt gained. The United States and the United Arab Emirates forgave Egypt $13.6 billion. Then Egypt was asked to conclude an agreement with the Club of Paris countries that resulted in waiving 50 percent of other debts, to be effected in stages (1992 and 1994), on the condition that Egypt implement the directives of the International Monetary Fund and the World Bank for what was called an 'economic reform program.' Through these arrangements, Egypt's foreign debt was reduced from $47.6 billion in June 1990 to $34 billion in February 1991 and then again to $24 billion in mid-1994, that is, to half of what it had been in mid-1990.

It is worth noting the relative stability of Egypt's foreign debt in the following ten years (1994–2004) compared to its sixfold increase during the ten years of Sadat's rule and another 60 percent rise during the first ten years of Mubarak's rule. From 1994 to 2004, Egypt's foreign debt increased by no more than $5.4 billion to reach $29.4 billion; that is by only 22 percent over ten years. Why this relative stability in Egypt's foreign debt after a quarter century of rapid increase?

One possible explanation is that it is not possible for any country to continue to borrow and to grow increasingly indebted forever. The time must come when a shortfall in debt service occurs and creditors begin to worry about their money. Then the debtor nation enters a new phase when it starts repaying more on past debts than it receives in new loans. Its indebtedness increases not when its economy grows weaker, but rather when the creditors are confident in its ability to repay. Creditors stop lending and demand repayment only when they lose confidence in the country's economic future. This happened with Khedive Ismail in the nineteenth century: lenders poured money into Egypt when the price of cotton was high during the American Civil War, then they began to tighten the noose once this era of prosperity ended. It happened again with Sadat: when lenders started drooling over elevated oil prices and large money transfers from Egyptian migrant workers in the Gulf, they lavished loans on Egypt, and then they tightened the noose around Mubarak when the price of oil fell and the migrant workers began coming home. But it is also possible to explain the relative stability in Egyptian indebtedness beginning in the early 1990s to this day by the decline in Egyptian growth rates along with the resulting decline in imports. The improvement in the balance of payments, as a result of reduced imports as well as the large reduction of the burden of debt service, freed Egypt from having to resort to more loans.

In any case, toward the end of the Mubarak era, foreign debt was no longer the pressing problem it had been at the beginning of his rule. By 2004, it represented no more than 31.2 percent of GDP, as opposed to 141 percent of GDP at the beginning of the Mubarak era, and debt service represented no more than 10 percent of the total value of Egypt's exports of goods and services, as compared with 28 percent in 1981. It seems that the worry over being in debt keeping one awake at night had been lifted (or nearly so); but the shame still persisted in the daytime, as the Egyptian saying goes. For Egypt is still subservient to the United States and continues to comply with American wishes and refrain from doing what the United States forbids her to do. Indeed, there is every indication that Egypt's subservience is much worse now than it was at the beginning of the Mubarak era.

This could be explained by a number of things. Getting you in debt is only one way of keeping you subservient. There is also the fear of scandal if someone is blackmailing you. There is the dependence on a foreign supply of weapons if one is unable to defend oneself. But there is also mere 'addiction.' If you have grown accustomed to a certain way of life as a result of your indebtedness, it becomes difficult to forgo it. A shopkeeper can lure you into his shop by encouraging you to buy now and pay later, to get whatever price he wants for his wares. But once you become addicted to his goods he no longer needs to offer you new loans.

Something like this seems to have happened to Egypt between the mid-1970s and the end of the 1980s, when the Open Door economic policy created new consumption habits among large segments of the upper and middle classes. Something similar may have happened to the Egyptian armed forces during the same time period, when they went from being armed with Soviet weaponry to being armed by the Americans. In both cases it was very difficult to turn back. Foreign loans had fulfilled their purpose and there was no more need to increase them for the time being.

As far as the economy is concerned, the Mubarak era may be said to have really started in the mid-1980s and not when Mubarak took office at the beginning of the decade. In the first five years (1981–85) the economy grew at the same high rate as that of the Sadat era (about 8 percent) and the same familiar weakness in economic structure also continued. The *infitah* endured unabated, the inflation rate remained high, as did the Egyptian migration rate to the oil states. The pattern of income distribution continued to be characterized by a large gap between income levels, even if migration created a breathing space for those of limited income.

In 1986 oil prices suddenly dropped, and Egyptian oil revenues declined, as did the rate of migration as a result of the decline in Gulf states' revenues. For both reasons the rate of unemployment rose. Matters were made worse when the International Monetary Fund intervened in 1987, forcing Egypt to adopt a Stabilization and Structural Adjustment Program. The Fund found an opportune moment to impose its conditions when it appeared that the Egyptian government was unable to service its debt. By way of debt restructuring, spreading out payments, and extending the repayment period, the Fund usually imposes on the debtor country an austerity program that obliges the government to reduce its expenditure (especially government subsidies for essential goods and services). This helps to bring down the inflation rate, but it also reduces the rate of growth in national output, increases unemployment, and adds to the burden of the poor.

That is exactly what happened in the following two decades, from 1986 to 2004: the growth rate of GDP did not exceed 4 percent on average, leading to a decline in the rate of growth of per capita income to less than 2 percent, noticeably less than what was realized in both the Sadat and Nasser eras (with the exception of those terrible eight years between the military defeat of 1967 and the beginning of the *infitah* era in 1974, a period that it is inappropriate to consider as representative of either the Nasser era or that of Sadat). The inflation rate duly fell in the decades between 1986 and 2004 from its level in the Sadat era because of the austerity policy, but the unemployment rate rose steeply, and incomes grew increasingly unequal. Some improvement, however, occurred in the economic structure in favor of manufacturing. But this last development requires an explanation.

Economists usually gauge the stage of a developing country's industrialization using three basic indicators: the change in the share of manufacturing industry in GDP, its share in the labor force, and its share in exports. As these indicators rise (with a corresponding fall in the share of agriculture, minerals, and services), the country is deemed more industrialized.

The industrialization effort during the 1950s and 1960s was highly satisfactory, especially between the mid-1950s and the mid-1960s, and the decade of the 1960s ended with Egypt being significantly more industrialized than it had been at the beginning of the decade. The share of manufacturing in GDP rose between 1960 and 1970 from 20 percent to 24 percent, while its share in the labor force increased from less than 10 percent to 14 percent, and its share of exports rose from 20 percent to 36 percent.

The rate of growth of manufacturing during the first half of the 1960s (years of the first five-year plan) was 8.5 percent, which would have been heralded as a great achievement had it been sustainable for another ten years. As it happened, the following decade was full of hardships, mostly as a result of the 1967 disaster, and industry did not begin to recover until the mid-1970s, when the growth rate fluctuated between 5.5 percent and 7.9 percent during the last five years of the Sadat era.

Industrial performance under Mubarak varied from one period to the next. Between 1981 and 1990 it was close to what it had been under Sadat, but it declined sharply until 1995; so much so that the growth rate of manufacturing in 1995–2000 was about half that of 1985–90 (5 percent and 10 percent respectively). It continued to decline until it fluctuated between 3 percent and 4 percent in the first years of the new century.

Despite this modest growth rate in industry during the Mubarak era, the share of manufacturing in GDP, labor force, and exports in 2005 was greater than it had been at the end of the Sadat era. It amounted to 20 percent of GDP (compared to 13.5 percent in 1981), 14 percent of the labor force (compared to 12.5 percent), and 45 percent of exports (compared to 9 percent). The explanation is, of course, that the growth of GDP declined steeply in the twenty years following 1986, as did oil prices compared to where they had been at the end of Sadat's presidency. Our three indicators for the progress of industrialization do not, therefore, give us a completely accurate picture of what really happened under Mubarak.

One other distinguishing feature of industrial development in the past five years has been the growing trend toward selling off the public sector. The industrial policy of the 1960s had been a mixture of building new industries from scratch and giving private firms (either foreign or Egyptian) over to public ownership. The talk of privatization began in the 1970s, but, throughout the 1970s and 1980s privatization was resisted stoutly by the Egyptian bureaucracy and industrial workers alike. In the 1990s the call for privatization became bolder, and the pressure from the IMF and the American administration to privatize increased after Egypt's signing of agreements with the Fund in May of 1991, and with the World Bank in November of the same year. It seems that by 2004 it was decided somewhere that privatization in Egypt should proceed at a much faster pace, a decision that brought to power a new type of government, in which the most prominent ministers were the keenest on selling off the public sector.

It is noteworthy that from the time the slogan of privatization was used in the 1970s, those using it kept quiet on the issue of whether the public sector companies would be sold to foreigners or to Egyptians. The word 'privatization' could, of course, include either form, since it merely means transferring public holdings to private hands. But there is a big difference between whether the new owners are Egyptian or foreigners. If they are Egyptian, the potential profits remain in the country and the government's ability to impose its conditions on the owners is greater, such as strict conditions to ensure that workers cannot be laid off or forced into early retirement without due respect for their rights, that consumers should not be subject to exploitation, or that the new buyer refrains from unduly harming the environment, and so on. International financial institutions such as the IMF and the World Bank usually refer to the benefits that would accrue from privatization as a result of 'increased efficiency,' but they have very little, if anything, to say about what the new owners might do with the assets they have purchased, or about how unlikely it is for the new buyers to commit themselves to higher social goals that are, in the end, the ultimate objectives of development. These institutions find it easy to assume that the state selling its holdings is a strong one, able to impose upon buyers the necessary conditions for the protection of national interests, and ignore their true nature: that they are soft states that would not have succumbed to selling their holdings in the first place had they not been so soft.

It is also worth noting that, throughout the 1985–2004 period, the amount of foreign investment in Egypt remained very small in spite of everything successive Egyptian governments did encourage that invest-ment, pinning their hopes upon it as the magic cure to Egypt's economic problems. To be sure, potential foreign investors and international orga-nizations were constantly complaining about the obstacles placed in their way by an incompetent, cumbersome, and corrupt bureaucracy, but I cannot be convinced that the dearth of foreign investment coming to Egypt during that period was really due to such impediments. When the rate of foreign investment in Egypt suddenly increased in 2005 no important change had occurred in any of these factors, and it was not really difficult for those interested in investing in Egypt to bring about the required changes by pressuring the government or even changing it if necessary. What seems more plausible a reason for the slow flow of investment to Egypt throughout this period is the prevailing political cli-mate in the Middle East.

Then, something seems to have happened in the summer of 2004, that is, a year after the U.S. occupation of Iraq and in the midst of a lot of talk about the need for a 'New Middle East.' That summer the gov-ernment of Egypt was suddenly changed and the new prime minister, Ahmad Nazif, was a man no one had expected to occupy the job and who had no known political history other than having been an undistinguished minister in the previous cabinet. The nature of the new government and the mission assigned to it soon became clear, however, once the names of those who would take over the ministries concerned with the economy, such as the ministries of Economy, Industry, the Treasury, Investment, Population, and Tourism, became known. All of them subscribed to a policy of unlimited economic liberalism, and all of them had pinned their hopes on private foreign investment and privatizing public enterprises. They were all keen to reduce or, better, to eliminate government subsidies on essential goods and services. With unfamiliar speed, the government took one step after another, aimed at opening the door wider to imports, more privatization, and subsidy reduction, and providing greater facilities to foreign firms.

Things became even clearer in December 2004 when Egypt signed an agreement with Israel and the United States establishing what were called the Qualifying Industrial Zones (QIZ, or Quiz), which allowed some Egyptian industrial firms (called 'qualified') entrance into the U.S. market duty-free on the condition that a minimum percentage of their inputs be of Israeli origin. Egyptian industry had thus started to be placed at the mercy of Israel, which is today able to dictate which industrial firms in Egypt should flourish and grow, and which should shrivel and die out.

In 2005, private foreign investment in Egypt doubled from the previous year and then doubled again over the next two years. When Arab potential investors saw this they understood what had happened and raced to invest and buy land in Egypt. The government was quick to announce that the GDP growth rate, which had remained fairly stationary at 4 percent for almost two decades, had risen to 7 percent or more, following the formation of the new government. This indicated, according to the government, that the period of gloom was over and that an era of rapid and sustainable development had begun; the success was attributed to the wisdom of the new government, compared to all previous governments, and it was as if all of the suffering of the Egyptian people over the previous twenty years had been the result of a simple error in the choice of the person to head the government, and of the ministers to work with him.

But while the new government was saying this, the Egyptian poor were fighting in lines in front of bakeries to get as much subsidized flatbread as they could. The size of the loaf had shrunk over time and its color had darkened, and in any case the owners of the bakeries were now refusing to hand out loaves in the numbers the poor were requesting.

4

The Poor

1

A few years ago I was on a train, returning to Cairo from Alexandria. About five minutes after the train had left the station, a young woman of about twenty-five entered the car carrying a pencil in one hand and a piece of paper in the other. She stopped at each row of seats and asked the passengers what they would like to have for dinner along the trip. This was not a new sight to me, but several things about this young woman caught my eye. She was neither pretty nor ugly, and there was nothing about her face that might attract attention except for the fact that it showed signs of misery. She looked as if she was doing what she was doing out of compulsion and with distaste, as if she would rather be anywhere else, doing anything else. Her clothes also attracted my attention. She wore a uniform, no doubt imposed upon her by the company operating the train or the one proffering the food: it was a suit, brown in color, but the skirt was shorter than was customary in those days, ending above the knee, and a pair of high heels, also unusual for young women in those days.

I did not have long to watch her because she came and went quickly. But no more than a few minutes passed before she returned with a man of about forty, similarly uniformed, pulling a trolley loaded with various drinks while the miserable young woman pushed it from the other end. This time they were offering drinks to the passengers, and the man was calling out, "juice, tea, coffee, Nescafé . . . ." Etched on his face were even deeper signs of wretchedness than those I had seen on the face of the young woman. He seemed utterly lost, spiritless, as though there was something on his mind besides what he was saying, or as if each time he uttered the names of his drinks he was asking his Lord why he'd been forced into doing this. On his forehead was the well-known callus (*zabiba*, or 'raisin') that develops as a result of frequent prostration in prayer, but his face did not convey any religiosity whatsoever. Instead, the despair that showed on his face revealed thoughts entirely to the contrary.

Nor was this look of despair new to me; indeed, I had begun seeing it whenever I left my home. For example, a short while before this train trip, I had stopped at a petrol station, which for many years had been a co-op station, but which had recently been bought by a multinational gas company. It had been repainted in bright red and yellow hues, and its attendants wore uniforms of the same flashy red and yellow. The first time I had stopped there after the changeover I was puzzled to find one of the attendants who filled the tank asking me to park to one side for a minute as he had a pleasant surprise for me. He asked me this in absolute earnest, which made it difficult to refuse. I did as he asked, whereupon a higher-ranked employee of the station approached to offer me a "gift from the station." I forget what it was, a book of coupons for discounts on my next petrol purchases or some fancy driving cushion. Whatever it was, I left hurriedly and in disgust, while the man called after me surprised and upset as if I had been a bird about to fall into his trap before escaping at the last moment and flying away. The next time I stopped at the station, another of the station's workers came over to try to sell me some oil or other fluid for the car at a special price. By then I was ready for him and refused the offer. He repeated it and I refused again; but he was determined and begged me with an unusual urgency to buy what he was offering. I lost my temper and scolded him severely, asking, "What do you think you're doing? Why are you begging me to buy this stuff? If you keep this up, I'll start looking for another petrol station and I'll never come back here again." When I looked at him, I saw an expression very similar to the one I had seen on the face of the young woman on the train: utter misery and despair barely concealed. He answered me in a pathetic tone of voice, saying that neither he nor any of his co-workers liked doing this and he fully understood what I meant. He promised to relay my message to a responsible party at the station. But I very much doubted that he would be bold enough to do it.

The same look of despair and misery that showed on the faces of the workers of these two companies which had so recently come to Egypt, I saw again on the faces of the veiled young women sitting behind the cash registers at a branch of a large supermarket. They had genuinely Egyptian features, but features that also betrayed their strong rural origins and their recent acquaintance with the city. So, too, did they betray a history of malnutrition (or so I thought). It was evident to me that the mega-company that owned the supermarket had recruited these young women from the poorest neighborhoods in Cairo, offering them wages they were unable to refuse, not because they offered them a decent standard of living, but because there was no other way open to these young women to obtain the necessities of life for themselves and perhaps for their families as well. Why, then, was such misery and despair written on their faces?

I recall that pretty young woman I had seen two or three years before, working as a waitress at a restaurant in one of the fancy international hotel chains on the Red Sea. The hotel was full of tourists of all nationalities, but I did not see a single Egyptian, other than those serving in it. This young woman was also wearing a very short skirt, but her clothing was much finer than the uniform worn by the young woman I saw on the train, and her hairstyle showed that a lot of effort had been devoted to it. Perhaps it was the hotel management that had insisted upon it. When she came over to my table I started a conversation. Asked about her salary, she named a sum equal to what a new graduate from the faculty of engineering of an Egyptian university might receive, but she complained of the long hours and how she had to go home every night to her family in the town of al-Quseir exhausted and unable to do anything but sleep. I started thinking about the frightening gulf that separated her life with her two parents and five of her siblings in al-Quseir, one of the poorest cities in Egypt, and the style of life in this beguiling hotel, with Swedish and Italian women running around near-naked in its hallways while she served bottles of wine to the guests in the restaurant. True, the salary was attractive to a young woman like her, and she could not have turned it down under any circumstances, but I did wonder if it could compensate for the sacrifice she was making.

It first occurred to me, when these and similar images of the poor in Egypt went through my mind, that all this was nothing other than the usual result of the wide gap between the rich and poor in Egypt; it had existed before the revolution and continued after it. But then I sensed that there was something different about the poor of today, something I noticed in those individuals I have mentioned, who served on trains, at the supermarket, the petrol station, and the fine hotel on the Red Sea, and which did not exist in the poor who I can still remember from before 1952. It's true that the pre-1952 poor were in an abject state and in some senses much worse off than the poor of today. But there are many kinds of poverty and deprivation, and the torment they give rise to is also of various types. Could it be that being deprived of enough food is sometimes less painful than, say, the inability to pay for private lessons for one's children? In any case, it seems to me that something must have happened to make the poor of Egypt feel their poverty and deprivation today much more intensely than they did fifty years ago, and even more than they felt before the 1952 revolution. What happened, exactly, to lead to this result?

2

Economists have a very simple conception of what causes poverty: low per capita income and unequal income distribution. The poor suffer when income growth slows down and income distribution becomes more unequal. But per capita income refers to the income of a theoretical person, neither very rich nor very poor, and can only be a very imperfect measure of what happens to this or that group of real people. As for income distribution, economists often use a measure called the Gini Coefficient, which gives the percentages of national income accruing to the highest, middle, and lowest percentile of the population. Thus, it might indicate, for example, that the richest 5 percent of the population used to receive 40 percent of national income but now receives only 30 percent, while the poorest 20 percent used to get 3 percent of national income but now gets 5 percent. This is taken as an improvement in income distribution, indicating an improvement in the state of the poor, but such figures tell us nothing about whether the poor may be suffering more or less than they had been. Their share of the national income may indeed have increased, but their needs or aspirations may have risen as well, making them more desperate. Alternatively, the behavior of the rich toward them may have become worse, causing the poor even greater frustration. Or their means of acquiring a greater share of the national income may have become more demeaning, causing them greater alienation. The list could go on.

It follows that the story of the poor in Egypt, if it were told in this manner, that is, as merely an account of changes in rates of growth and in income distribution, must surely ignore very important things that have happened in Egypt over the past fifty years, the last twenty years in particular. The poor of today are not the poor of yesterday, and the things they feel a powerful need for are not the same things they needed fifty years or even a quarter century ago. So, too, do the rich, whom the poor see everywhere and compare themselves with, seem to be of a different type from the rich of yesterday. The poor today are not, as they were in the past, simply people with depressed incomes; a large and growing proportion of them are people without any income at all, as they are unemployed. And unemployment is not only a cause of poverty, but brings with it other things that may be worse than poverty. But whether unemployed or not, the poor today think more of the future than they did fifty years ago, and they find it more of a cause for worry than they did before. The Egyptian poor of today find their deprivation sharper and crueler than it used to be. All this all needs to be elaborated and explained, something that economists usually do not attempt.

3

Before the revolution, poverty was essentially a rural phenomenon. Thus the first people to come to mind when the issue of poverty arose were the 'poor of the countryside.' More than 80 percent of the population in Egypt was living off agriculture, the great majority in abject poverty as small sharecroppers or agricultural laborers. Nowadays, the rural population has shrunk to about 50 percent, and the urban lifestyle has reached the rural villages to the extent that the features of village poverty have become very similar to those of urban poverty. Thus the problem of poverty in Egypt has gradually transformed to become essentially the problem of the urban poor.

It has been generally accepted, at least since writers described the conditions of the poor in British cities during the industrial revolution, that urban poverty could be much more cruel than rural poverty. Essential goods and services that the poor must pay for in the city are usually more than those in the countryside, where many of them are available for free or at much-reduced prices. Urban life imposes new financial strains upon city dwellers that were not necessary in the village, such as transportation costs, while living alone in a city often requires new expenses that were once borne by the whole family or may require means of entertainment for which there was little need in a rural society. Generally, it can be said that people's needs, be they rich or poor, are greater in the city than they are in the countryside; spending to meet them is also higher in the city, as is the frustration felt at failing to meet them, and the alienation, humiliation, and loss of self esteem. Egyptians have been increasingly exposed to such hardships with the growth in the percentage of the population residing in cities throughout the last fifty years, but some periods were harder for the urban poor than others, and there are several indications that the past twenty years have been worse than those before them.

In the ten years between 1956 and 1966, the hardships facing Egyptian migrants from the villages to the cities were relatively easy to deal with. For one thing, there does not appear to be a great difference between what Egyptians considered to be basic necessities at the end of that period and what they did at its beginning. This is true of items of food or clothing, what was deemed an appropriate dwelling or an acceptable level of education, health care, means of transportation, and types of entertainment. The economic policy followed at the time did not permit importing fine foods or high-priced clothing either, except under the tightest restrictions. So, too, was everyone obliged to use the same locally available materials for building and furnishing their home. It was impossible, no matter how rich one was, to import deluxe bathrooms or electrical appliances such as refrigerators, stoves, vacuum cleaners, fans, or air conditioners. The choice was either to use what was available (and largely made) locally or nothing at all. Anyone who was able to do otherwise was as good as a smuggler, whether he was caught out or not. And very rare was the person bold enough to try.

Nor was there in those days the abundance of foreign language schools in Egypt that we see today, and indeed even the schools that had been foreign before had become Egyptianized. In fact, we had very few private schools at that time. Similarly, there was hardly any of what are now called 'investment hospitals,' which possess the newest equipment and instruments, and charge the highest prices. Nor was there the lavish spending on the 'rich and famous,' which we know today as 'medical treatment abroad at state expense.' Ownership of private cars was still confined to a small percentage of Egyptians, and most government officials, even in high positions, were using the Nasr 1100 car, which was manufactured in Egypt.

Sources of entertainment also underwent amazingly little change during that period. It is true that television came to Egypt at the beginning of the 1960s, but for a number of years Egyptian television remained a very solemn affair, broadcasting for only a few hours a day and ending with the national anthem at midnight. It had only a handful of channels and no advertisements. It would frequently broadcast the patriotic songs of the immensely popular singer 'Abd al-Halim Hafez, some of which referred to the building of the High Dam and even to the five-year plan.

The middle class would go to the seaside in the summer, as they had always done, and for most Egyptians that meant going to Alexandria. The development of the North Coast had not yet been conceived; and, in any case, that would have required the possession of a car, which remained rare until the 1970s. Travel abroad for fun was greatly limited by the very small amount of Egyptian pounds people were allowed to exchange into foreign currencies.

All this, which may seem strange now, was for the most part due to the restrictions imposed by the government at the time on imports of all kinds. Admittedly, the whole world had not yet entered the age of the 'consumer society,' which caused a great transformation in what are regarded as 'the necessities of life.' But when the world, or more precisely the western world, entered this new age around the mid-1960s, Egypt was to embark on a very depressing decade for rich and poor alike.

For, in the ten years following the defeat of 1967, the rate of growth of national income as well of per capita income declined sharply, and imports continued to be severely restricted, not so much for the purpose of protecting Egypt's infant industry, as it had been in the previous decade, but simply because of limited means. Egyptian cities suffered greatly from the government's reduced ability to spend on badly needed maintenance of roads, sewerage systems, mass transit, and the telephone service. At the same time, the government continued to bear the responsibility for furnishing jobs to those asking for them, as it had done in the preceding ten years, but in this period its ability to make new investments was greatly weakened, and few new jobs were available outside government employment. In such a climate no real opportunity existed to improve the lot of the poor, nor was there any great opportunity for the rich to increase their wealth.

It was in the following decade (1976–86) that a huge transformation occurred in the lives of both the rich and poor of Egypt: in what they regarded as indispensable goods and services, and in their patterns of expenditure. An urgent desire came over Egyptians to fulfill needs that they may have never heard of before. This was the result of opening the doors wide to imports at a time when the whole world was opening up and succumbing to feverish campaigns encouraging greater consumption.

The cost of fulfilling these new 'needs' took a great leap upward with the arrival of runaway inflation: the inflation rate in Egypt has multiplied threefold since the 1950s and 1960s. Something similar happened all over the world, but the *infitah* turned Egypt into a leaf blown by a wind from the outside world.

A revolution overcame Egyptian television; the black-and-white set became colored, the number of channels multiplied, and the hours of operation were extended. Television entered almost every house in Egypt, with every man, woman, and child, educated or uneducated, learning to sit in front of it for hours, day and night. It occupied a prime place in the coffee houses, and then it slipped out of the cities into the villages. A color television became the poor Egyptian's dream; for its sake people went into debt or sold off their jewelry, economizing on food and clothing if necessary, paying in cash on the barrelhead or on the installment plan, while wives demanded a divorce if their husbands could not afford one. When television grew widespread, advertisement became a very lucrative business, turning into an essential part of every television program.

Such change increased in power and speed with the increasing migration of Egyptian workers to the Gulf. As already mentioned, inflation and the scarcity of job opportunities within Egypt pushed large numbers of workers to the oil-rich states, if not for the amassing of a fortune then at least to earn enough money to buy a color television set and a Japanese-made fan. But migration, and the increase in remittances sent to Egypt, helped to raise the rate of inflation, which pushed others to migrate, and so on, in a vicious circle. In the process, those who managed to travel for work, and those who did not, acquired new habits, including coveting new goods and lifestyles that had not been affordable or even known to Egyptians before.

Ambition and covetousness grew stronger, but migration, or even the mere chance to migrate, strongly reduced the feelings of frustration. Ambitions were high, and the chance of working abroad gave large numbers of the poor the hope that they might fulfill them. While inflation increased people's worry about what the future held, the hope of finding work in the Gulf blunted the edge of this worry. One might tell oneself, "I'll go abroad for work and save for the children," or, "the children will get an education and then find jobs abroad." Migration from the village to the city became just a first step toward migrating to one of the oil-rich states. The rural migrant to the city, be it an Egyptian city or a city in a Gulf state, would of course feel alienated in the midst of such a flood of new goods that he could ill afford, but he carried within himself the hope that one day he might be able to participate in the enjoyment of it all.

All of this began to change in the mid-1980s, when deep frustration began to replace high ambition, and feelings of despair, coupled with greater fear for the future, started to spread. The sense of alienation grew more oppressive when hopes started to fade.

4

I have many reasons for believing that the years between 1986 and 2006 have been among the worst in the lives of the Egyptian poor, not just in the last fifty years, but perhaps in the entire twentieth century. Yes, there was some rise in per capita income; the inflation rate was lower—on average—than it had been in the previous decade (1976–86), and the income distribution figures, even if they indicate a deterioration during the last twenty years, at least do not show a very sharp increase in inequality. Nevertheless, there are many important things, which I have already referred to, that are not easily measured, and in fact may be impossible to measure, but tend to make the feeling of deprivation much more oppressive. Some essential goods and services have grown farther out of reach, some things once considered luxuries have come to be considered necessary, and the burden of meeting these needs has grown heavier. Worry over what the future could bring has grown, and the feeling of alienation has also grown stronger. How did all this happen?

This twenty-year period began with two significantly negative events: a large and sudden reduction in the price of oil and increased pressure from the International Monetary Fund (IMF) on the Egyptian government to reduce its role in the economy in the interests of the poor. The drop in oil prices was something that the Egyptian state could do nothing about, but the IMF influence was the result of both an external will and internal folly: the Fund certainly made use of the opportunity presented by the Egyptian government's inability to service its large foreign debts, caused by some foolish economic decisions taken in the previous ten years.

The poor of Egypt suffered far more than the rich from the effects of these two developments. The fall in the price of oil led to the return of many Egyptian migrants, most of whom belonged to the low-income groups, to whom were added tens of thousands of Egyptians who returned as a result of Saddam Hussein's invasion of Kuwait in 1990. The poor who had not left Egypt but who were hoping to do so were obliged to put off their travel for an indefinite period and join the ranks of the unemployed. The fall in oil prices also led to a fall in Egyptian government revenues coming from both the export of oil and the Suez Canal. This, combined with the pressure from the IMF, caused a large decline in government services as well as subsidies to education, health services, housing, and transportation. The poor found themselves obliged to bear the burden of these reduced subsidies at a time when incomes were rising at a very slow pace and work opportunities were becoming increasingly scarce.

Unemployment was not, of course, a new phenomenon in Egypt, but until the mid-1980s it was mainly of the kind known to economists as 'disguised unemployment,' which means working at extremely low productivity for extremely low wages. Before the revolution, a typical example of this was a poor rural family of, say, eight people, working a small plot of land that needs no more than two or three farm hands. Another example was a street vendor calling out to people to buy his goods, which, if he managed to sell them all, would allow him only a minimum income.

In contrast, 'open unemployment' refers to not having a job at all, in spite of the existence of the desire and ability to work. This type of unemployment was very rare in Egypt before the 1952 revolution because of the relatively small size of the manufacturing sector and because education was not yet widespread enough to produce a greater number of graduates or school leavers than available jobs. In the years between 1956 and 1966 both disguised and open unemployment declined because of the efforts of the revolution in accelerating industrial development and introducing land reform, which accommodated many more workers in agriculture than there had previously been. Unemployment increased during the following decade (1966–76), owing to the decrease in investments following the 1967 war, but this was followed by another dip in unemployment of both types during the decade 1976–86 as a result of migration. From 1986 unemployment started to increase for the reasons given above, and have gone on increasing to this day.

Official unemployment figures in recent years greatly underestimate the size of the problem, not only because of the very narrow definition of being 'unemployed,' but also because they do not take into account those people who have jobs that are completely out of line with their qualifications—like an engineer who works as a taxi driver, a law school graduate working as a hotel receptionist, or a holder of a commercial school certificate working as a housemaid or cashier in a supermarket. No one of these is counted in the Egyptian official statistics as unemployed, but they all could be as miserable as any unemployed person.

The same thing may be said of many Egyptian women who are compelled to work outside the house. Of course, they also do not appear in the unemployment statistics, even though they may have been pushed to work by the continuing unemployment or low wages of their husbands. This is not disguised unemployment, for their hours of work may be long and their productivity quite high compared with the street vendors or most government employees, but it could carry a much heavier psychological burden than either open or disguised unemployment.

For this and other reasons, one should not attach too great a significance to the results of labor market surveys published by some official agency at the end of October 2006, claiming that the unemployment situation in Egypt had shown noticeable improvement between 1998 and 2006. It was clear from reading the results, first that this "noticeable improvement" did not include greater Cairo, and hence the recorded "improvement" was supposed to have taken place in the countryside. But this may very well have been the result of migration to greater Cairo in search of jobs without success. Secondly, this "improvement" in rural unemployment might also have been caused by the fact that those who had been unemployed for too long had finally despaired of finding work and decided to accept any job on offer.

Meanwhile, some other strange things have been happening during the last twenty years to increase the agony felt by the poor. The fortunes accumulated during the first decade of the *infitah* (1976–86) had indeed attracted a lot of attention, with many amazing stories being told about the sudden rise in the wealth of currency traders, contractors, or landlords renting furnished apartments, and about the ostentatious weddings such nouveaux riches would throw at the large hotel chains, simply for the sake of showing off the huge wealth they had recently made. All this, however, did not stir the frustration of the poor as the accumulated riches of the following twenty years did. The growth in wealth in the earlier period was accompanied by the increase in the ability of a significant portion of the poor to migrate to the Gulf, and many of those who did not migrate benefited from the general increase in wage levels coupled with generous spending on the part of the state. In fact, a sudden increase in wealth at that time inspired more scorn and sarcasm than frustration. This cannot be said of the following twenty years, when examples of wealth accumulation became rather obscene, and all doors were closed to the poor, educated and uneducated alike.

Among the features of this obscene wealth was that one of its main sources came to be the appropriation of public property. In a period when incomes are rising all around (such as the period 1976–86), it is possible to get rich quickly without usurping other people's property, but, in a period of relative economic stagnation, as was the case in the following twenty years (1986–2005), few chances exist for getting rich except by plundering already existing assets. The easiest way to achieve this under a soft state is to put one's hands on state property, including state lands offered for sale, or loans extended by public sector banks, or the assets of a public sector company subject to privatization. Such deeds became known to everyone, and the feelings of anger and frustration grew.

Meanwhile, television channels never ceased to broadcast provocative images—real or imaginary—of the happiness that wealth can bring. Over the last twenty years, Egyptian television has greatly increased its power to deceive, while no attention has been paid to what should or should not be displayed in a poor country such as Egypt. People were shown an on-screen lifestyle that the majority of them could not even dream of attaining. As the power and influence of advertisers grew, advertising came to occupy the most important prime-time slots on television. It did not take long for those supervising Egyptian television to lose all power over what Egyptians could watch, especially after the introduction of satellite networks to Egypt and their phenomenal spread in cities and villages. All this must be part of the explanation for that look of despair that I keep seeing on the faces of many of today's employees.

5

Egypt's Information and Decision Support Center, attached to the cabinet of ministers, was established to provide the cabinet with necessary data and research on important issues. In April 2006, the director of this center made a statement in which he vigorously denied the allegation that the poor in Egypt were getting poorer. The evidence he gave for this, which he thought irrefutable, was that owners of refrigerators in Egypt had risen from 56 percent of Egyptian families to 87 percent between 1995 and 2005. He said that similar observations could be made of fixed telephones and mobile phones, and of expenditure on various means of communication. He added that this meant that conditions had not worsened for Egyptians, who had greater aspirations and had grown more ambitious.

Reading this statement, it occurred to me that it might be better for the Center to rely on indicators other than the ownership of refrigerators or mobile phones, such as the amount of meat an Egyptian family consumed in a week or a year, the ability to buy or rent accommodation—and hence to get married,[6] the conditions of public transport available to the Egyptian poor, the level of education or the extent of the need for private lessons to compensate for the deterioration of school education, or the quality of the health care available to them and to their families.

In my boyhood (that is, in the late 1940s and early 1950s), the ability to buy a refrigerator may indeed have been a good indicator of a family's belonging to the middle class and of its ability to meet its basic requirements. But the situation has changed greatly since then so that the possession of a refrigerator is no longer a sign of lessening poverty. The reason for this is simple: the big change that has occurred over the last fifty years in the relative cost of various goods and services. The prices of many essential goods have increased at a rate much greater than that of such things as refrigerators and other durable goods. The result is that it is no longer the possession of a refrigerator that counts but rather what it has inside it.

To illustrate the point, toward the end of the 1940s the cost of a refrigerator of average quality in Egypt relative to the monthly salary of a new college graduate was about 1:15. Today the ratio is about 1:6. In other words, a new graduate today needs to spend about six months' salary or less to buy a refrigerator while he needed to work for fifteen months to get one sixty years ago. The opposite has occurred with the prices of more necessary items, such as meat. While a university graduate at the end of the 1940s could buy with his monthly salary about sixty kilograms of meat; today he can only buy five or six kilograms. What applies to refrigerators applies to many other durable goods like televisions and mobile phones, the prices of which have tended to drop relative to income. Similarly, what applies to the price of meat applies, too, to the prices of vegetables, pulses, and fruit (and one may also add potable water), as well as to the cost of education and health care.

6

On the first day of Eid al-Fitr, or the 'Small Feast,' in November 2006, a shocking incident occurred in downtown Cairo, leading many to feel that a new and perilous development had come about in the lives of Egyptians. Dozens (some say hundreds) of young men reportedly began attacking women in the streets, sexually harassing them and in some cases tearing their clothes off, all before the eyes of onlookers, including policemen. The incident occurred only a few days after we heard that the drinking water of a number of Egyptian cities and villages was polluted and came from the sewers, sending several people to hospital. The question that passed through my mind was this: could the explanation for what happened in downtown Cairo be the deterioration of the quality of life for many Egyptians to a level that is not really fit for human existence? Could it be the decline of educational standards, of job availability, and of housing suitable for humans such that they might marry and have a decent life? Is this the reason why many young Egyptians have been pushed to wander hopelessly about in the streets, seeking sexual gratification by rubbing up against women in mass transit vehicles (and now in the streets) or through common-law marriages that they know have no legal standing?

These young men seem to have nothing to lose, not a wife, children, or a good job, and have little hope in the foreseeable future of gaining any of these. Nor are they concerned with the opinions of the people around them, whether their actions inspire revulsion or contempt. They feel insignificant and despised anyway because they have nothing to distinguish them from tens of thousands of other young men straying about the streets. Nor do they have anything to fear from the police, when the policemen themselves seem scarcely different from these lost souls. Take a look at those policemen and at the expressions of helplessness on their faces, their emaciated bodies marked by malnutrition, their excessive humility making them unable to scare away a fly, much less a pack of youths hounding women in the street.

7

On the morning of 18 April 2006, a lorry carrying stones and gravel struck a vehicle carrying fifteen young girls between the ages of sixteen and eighteen. The girls were on their way to a secondary technical school in the town of Atfih, fifty miles south of Cairo. All of them died. People wondered who might be responsible for the deaths of these girls. Was it the lorry driver who said that he had to swerve to avoid hitting an old woman? Was it the owner of the vehicle that carried the girls? According to statements made by the girls' families, "the owners of such vehicles sit around at coffee houses, renting them out to young, unlicensed drivers, and the vehicles themselves, which were originally intended for transporting livestock, are neither numbered nor licensed."

Or is the responsible party the governor or the cabinet minister who did not respond to repeated requests from the inhabitants of the village to open a school closer to their homes, so that their children would not be forced to ride livestock trucks to and from a school more than twenty kilometers away? More perplexing is that a decision to build such a school had indeed been taken in 2003 but was never implemented. Should the finger of blame point to those responsible for road maintenance in Egypt, with all of their speed bumps that serve no apparent purpose, and with no sidewalks on which elderly men and women might walk?

Or could it be possible that the responsibility should be laid at the door of the girls themselves or their families, who knew quite well the danger they were exposing themselves to by riding in such a vehicle and going to school standing in an overloaded flatbed truck driven by an inexperienced, unlicensed driver? Moreover, many other accidents of a similar sort had occurred along the same route, in which some relatives of these same girls had died, including the brother of one of them, only a year and a half before and in a similar accident. Or might not the guilty party be the person or persons who, even though it constitutes one of their responsibilities, are unconcerned about the growing problem of unemployment in Egypt, such that it forces some young people to work as drivers without a license?

There are several other people beside those mentioned who could be considered responsible for the accident. Thus, I was utterly amazed when I read in the papers that a judge of Southern Giza had remanded the driver in the accident of killing fifteen girls in Atfih. I asked myself, "Could it be true, in the light of all I have just mentioned, that the lorry driver was the real cause of the accident? Did he really commit all of those crimes attributed to him: causing accidental death, injury, and unintentional damage, driving without a license, fleeing the scene of an accident, and failing to give proper aid to the victims?"

Before two weeks had passed after these charges were laid, a sentence of ten years' imprisonment was passed on the lorry driver. The judge said he had passed the sentence "on the basis of the large number of aggrieved parties." *Al-Ahram* published news of the ruling with the headline, "Sentence Putting an End to Spilling Blood on the Asphalt," speculating that such a sentence "might deter those who play with the lives of the innocent on the roads." It reported that the families of the victims "assembled before the courthouse early in the day, eagerly following the trial of the driver who had killed their own flesh and blood." This is how the media put a decisive end to the subject, ruling that the driver was the guilty party, that it was he who had "played with the lives of the innocent," and reporting that the families were content with the sentence, which "granted them their revenge."

5

The Pashas

In our younger days we used to laugh at what we would sometimes hear about what happened between King Farouk and his friends. For amusement he would jokingly address as 'Pasha' one of his retinue, or even an ordinary citizen who happened to be lucky enough to meet the king, and the man would then suddenly become a real pasha. For, in those days, anything that was uttered by the king was considered a command, and whatever the king ordered became reality.

In that way, many people who came in contact with the king for one reason or another won the title of pasha or bey. But, aside from such occasional incidents, it was known to be a consistent practice throughout the monarchical era that the king would only bestow the title of pasha on high officials of state and the title of bey on some lower-ranking employees. Anyone other than those would remain merely 'effendi' if he had the luck to be educated and to wear European dress, 'sheikh' if he wore the traditional caftan, and 'osta' if he were a tradesman.

But because the high officials were at the same time and almost without exception large landowners, the title of pasha was associated in the minds of the people throughout the monarchy with significant agricultural land holdings. It was unimaginable that there might be a poor pasha, or even one of moderate income. A pasha was always rich, and the source of his riches was ownership of agricultural land, indeed it had to be an extensive holding.

For that reason, when, in the last days of his monarchy, King Farouk bestowed the title of pasha on the leading Egyptian writer of the time, Taha Hussein (after he became minister of education in the last Wafd government), it seemed to us a very strange thing indeed. To hear the name Taha Hussein associated with the title of pasha sounded rather odd. Taha Hussein Pasha? With all due respect to Taha Hussein, was he really from that class to which the pashas belonged?

Aside from their wealth, the pashas in those days were members of the ruling class; their words were listened to and their orders obeyed, not simply because the majority of the ministers and prime ministers were from the same class, but also because their great wealth was in itself a source of power and influence. A calling card carrying a pasha's name and title was usually enough to win its carrier a small government post or some means of livelihood, without the need for any prior meeting between the pasha and the person responsible for the decision. Why not appoint this person? Has he not come recommended by a pasha?

None of this was odd in a semi-feudal society. There was hardly any other source of wealth than agriculture, and there was almost no way of increasing wealth except by owning more agricultural land. Industry formed a trivial part of the national product, and those who had become rich through industry were only a small handful. No wonder that when Ahmed Abbud, who became rich through industrial property, was granted the title, the association between his name and pasha seemed as strange as the association of the name of Taha Hussein with the same title.

Thus it was surprising how quickly this changed after the July Revolution. It was not unexpected that the revolution would cancel all titles only a few months after coming to power, and replace them all with a plain 'Mr.' in all official addresses and transactions. What *was* strange was how quickly people grew accustomed to the new situation, and the speed with which they forgot the old titles and willingly gave them up.

The reason for this must have been the severe attack that the revolution launched on the men of the previous era, which was often referred to as the 'bygone era,' and the frequent references to the corruption of the old pashas and their ruinous impact on political life. The title 'pasha' soon became an object of scorn or mockery, and everybody welcomed the title of 'Mr.' in the prevailing atmosphere of equality and class leveling.

There was another reason, no less important, for the decline in value of the title, and this was the relative decline in the place of agriculture and landholdings as a source of wealth compared to other sources of income, especially industry. As already mentioned, the revolution raised the banner of economic development, and development was considered synonymous with industrialization. The main source of the high growth rate after the revolution was the rapid growth in industry and services. And in industry and services there are no pashas; both rest on the shoulders of professionals and workers. The professionals had rarely been beys, much less pashas, and there were not even effendis among the workers.

So the title 'The honorable Mr.' spread, and people accepted it willingly, finding nothing amiss in forgetting the two old titles. We thought at the time that they had vanished forever, but we were being extravagant in our optimism. Before long, the title pasha was back with us and even with renewed vigor. The title is now used with noticeable frequency. We hear it used to address the duty officer at the police station, or the high-ranking officers of the police or the army, in fact to address any official at all, as long as the person speaking to him is of a lower rank. We hear it used when talking to the owner of an apartment building, to the head of a government agency, or to the owner of a factory, shop, or restaurant; to say nothing of a cabinet minister, his deputy, and his associates, regardless of their social origin.

What they all have in common is power. A pasha now is not an owner of vast agricultural land; instead he is a person who has power over somebody beneath him. It is true that today's pasha, aside from being in a position of power, is also a rich man, but his riches now, contrary to what they were in the past, are the result of his power, whereas in the past it was the other way round.

It is also true that the use of the title 'pasha' has always been an expression of social hierarchy. That hierarchy was first based on land ownership, but this received a severe blow in the 1950s and 1960s as a result of land and income redistribution. But it began to return gradually, timidly at first in the 1960s, when a new social hierarchy began to emerge based upon proximity to power. In the 1970s, social hierarchy came to be based on whether one profited or lost from the *infitah*, migrated or did not migrate to an oil-producing country, or whether one managed to get rich with inflation or was beaten down by it. By the 1980s and 1990s another basis for social hierarchy was added, which was the ability to get one's hands on state property.

This change in hierarchy can explain the change in the meaning given to the title of pasha and in the intonation with which it is used. Its use has always expressed a certain distinction in rank, but it did not previously carry with it the degree of subservience that we often see today. Calling someone pasha in the past was very much a statement of fact; that was when a pasha was really a pasha, and he was addressed with the title without necessarily invoking any haughtiness in the one being addressed or obsequiousness in the one addressing him. Now the title is used most often when begging for a favor or pleading for mercy in the use of power. No wonder the title 'pasha' is today more associated with a feeling of humiliation and self-debasement than ever before.

6

The Middle Class

1

The middle class in Egypt today is a defeated and humiliated class. No wonder it also has little enthusiasm for national issues and its productivity is low in both the economic and cultural spheres. Things were not always this way. There was a time in the life of this class when it felt itself clearly distinguished from the lower class; it was very self-confident, aware of its own worth, full of hopes for itself and the country, politically active, and highly productive in the cultural arena.

In this chapter I trace some important changes that came over the Egyptian middle class starting from the pre-revolutionary era, through the eras of Nasser and Sadat, and up to the past few years of the Mubarak era, hoping to discover the causes of the deterioration in the living conditions of this class upon which hopes are usually pinned for national revival, considering that the lower classes do not have the means, and the upper class does not have the motivation to bring about such a revival.

At the time of the July 1952 revolution, the Egyptian middle class was indeed quite small in size, but it was quite distinct, patriotic, and highly influential. The middle class did not constitute, at that time, more than 20 percent of the population; the great majority, or slightly less than 80 percent, consisted of poor peasants, leaving a tiny percentage, perhaps no more than 1 percent, as an upper class. The middle class had doubled in size during the first half of the twentieth century, from about 10 to 20 percent of the total population, following very slow growth throughout the preceding century. The significantly rapid growth came after the 1952 revolution. But, in spite of its small size before 1952, the Egyptian middle class was distinguished in every meaning of the word.

First, there was the ease with which its members could be differentiated from other classes, such that one could almost identify a member of the middle class by appearance alone. Wearing European-style dress along with the tarboosh[7] was enough at that time to mark a person as middle class, for it was very rare for someone of the lower class to dress in that manner. Indeed, even to be wearing shoes was almost enough for such distinction as the large majority of people from the lower class went barefoot. The same was true for middle-class women, who wore skirts and dresses rather than the *gallabiya* or *milayat laff* worn by the poorer classes.[8] Members of the upper class did not often appear in public, but when they did they were recognizable by the European-tailored clothing worn by the pashas and members of the royal family—by things such as the shape of the collar or the manner of knotting the tie, the appearance of the shoes, and so on.

The middle class was also distinguished by its education, something not evident in appearance, but which quickly becomes clear in speech, and even in the exchange of greetings. It was very rare to find an uneducated person among the middle class, just as it was rare to find one living a life of privation. True, there might be a successful but illiterate merchant, or the owner of a profitable workshop who was also illiterate, or an illiterate person owning five feddans of land or more; but all of these were very rare. Hence, belonging to the middle class in people's perceptions meant having had an education, and an education was almost a sufficient condition for entering into the middle class.

The barrier separating the countryside and the city also represented a much greater divide between two income levels than we see nowadays. Of course, there were poor people in the cities, and some rich people in the countryside; but the poor represented a much smaller percentage of the total urban population than they do today, and the rich in the countryside also represented a much smaller proportion of the populations of villages and provincial towns than they do today. Middle-class houses did need their domestic workers, but the servants usually lived in the same houses that they served. Egypt did not yet have domestic servants who work only during certain hours of the day. Industrial workers, whose growth in the west had been the main reason for the growth of the urban poor, were very limited in number in Egypt before the revolution because of the slow growth of industry.

The Egyptian middle class had its preferred means of transportation. The private automobile had not yet become widespread and it was easy to differentiate between those owned by the few members of the upper class and those of the middle class that did use them. Private chauffeurs were common, for the wage of a chauffeur had not risen beyond the means of the middle class to pay them. At the same time, members of the middle class did not find it beneath themselves to ride the tram, metro, or bus. The fares of even these three modes of transportation, to say nothing of taxis, were, however, too high for the poor. Meanwhile, the train was an important means of transportation for all three classes. Each train comprised three classes of travel, each quite distinct from the other, just as the three social classes were distinct from each other. First class was almost always nearly empty, used only by the pashas and such people; the few second-class cars, with their leather seats, were used almost exclusively by the middle class; while the people from the lower classes would crowd into the numerous third-class cars, sitting on the spare wooden benches with their children, their coarse, palm-fiber baskets (sing. *quffa*),[9] and their palm-stalk fowl cages (sing. *qafas*).

Similar observations may be made of means of entertainment: the middle class mostly went to the theater and concert halls; the Egyptian cinema was mostly limited to an urban audience drawn from the upper strata of the lower class or the lower strata of the middle class, for the upper strata of the middle class as well as the upper class preferred Hollywood films, finding Egyptian ones to be too puerile. Most members of the lower classes found their entertainment in the many diversions of saints' festivals (sing. *mulid*) and other religious gatherings. The radio was very rare in the countryside, where there was no electricity to speak of until mid-century; and it was rare even among lower-class inhabitants of the cities. Thus, radios and, later, television sets were some of the consumer goods that distinguished middle-class houses from those of the lower classes.

The middle class was also distinguished by its strong patriotism. I certainly do not mean to deny the existence of patriotic sentiment in other classes, but there are important reservations about the strength of this feeling among the upper and the lower classes, even though the reasons for these reservations differ greatly between the two classes.

The upper class before the revolution was composed of a large proportion of persons of Turkish origin, among whom there was a widespread spirit of condescension toward Egyptians, whom they often referred to as 'peasants,' along with a strong admiration for and inclination to imitate the west, strengthened, no doubt, by the desire to differentiate themselves from the rest of the people, which they certainly had the means to do.

For their part, the sense of patriotism felt by the lower class was weakened both by their poverty and by their lack of education. Most of this class consisted of peasants, to whom could be applied the statement of Karl Marx that "the proletariat has no nation" even more than it could be to the proletariat of Marx's time. The difficulties faced in just trying to remain alive, not to mention the difficulties in gaining access to information that would connect them to the rest of the world, made them little concerned about such things as political independence or national progress.

Members of the middle class on the other hand saw British soldiers and officers parading before their eyes in the streets of the capital and other major cities; they could see the monopoly on trade and what little there was of industry held by foreigners, and they felt the domination of foreigners over the political life of their country. They had received a fine education that had acquainted them well with the history of the Egyptian national movement, and this caused them to feel a responsibility toward a continued national struggle.

This was the class that, a third of a century before the 1952 revolution, had staged the revolution of 1919, and had demanded and gained some degree of political independence in 1922, and a highly advanced constitution in 1923. It was the class that established Bank Misr and its industries, and demanded and obtained measures for the protection of Egyptian industry in the 1930s and 1940s. It is no wonder that this Egyptian middle class was, during the first half of the twentieth century, also highly productive in the cultural arena. Admittedly, its role in the economic sphere was limited to its planting the seeds of some new industries in the interwar period, but it was unable to continue along this road because of the restrictions placed upon Egyptian industrialization by the British occupation. But in the cultural domain this class managed to reach a level of excellence that Egypt had not come near to producing either before or after that period. It founded the Egyptian University in

1908; an active Society for Writing, Translation, and Publishing in 1914; and published two highbrow weekly journals (*al-Risalah* and *al-Thaqafa*), which had a profound impact on intellectual life from the early 1930s until their closure in the early 1950s. It also produced beautiful works of music, theater, cinema, sculpture, and painting, and led successful movements of religious, literary, artistic, and linguistic revival. What, then, was the impact of the July Revolution on the Egyptian middle class that had borne all of these fruits?

2

Nasser extended an important service to the Egyptian middle class by contributing to its vigorous growth through two channels: on the one hand he made it possible for large numbers from the lower class to enter the middle class by way of education, vocational training, or through acquiring government or public sector jobs, and through the impact of agricultural reform on small landholders and tenant farmers; on the other, Nasser expelled numbers of the upper class from their comfortable positions, obliging them to join the ranks of the middle class.

But, at the same time, the very steps that led to the growth of the middle class also resulted in a weakening of its distinguishing features. As I have said, the middle class had been slow to grow before the revolution, and the means for entering it came mainly in the form of education. In the two decades following the revolution, the rise into the middle class was much faster than it had been. Hence, the lingering effects of a rural upbringing remained with the new members of the class, even if some of them managed to reach the highest position within it. Education remained an important source of upward social mobility in the 1950s and 1960s, but the degree of attainment within the class was not as firmly fixed to level of education as it had been before the revolution. It became possible to quickly gain wealth and influence through proximity to the founders of the revolution, or by establishing one's trustworthiness and skill in the types of work that the revolution now required, even if such skills were not acquired through formal education.

As we have seen, the revolution abolished titles, and the sobriquets pasha, bey, and effendi almost disappeared, to be replaced by 'the honorable Mr.' as a term of address. But the title 'Mr.' does not distinguish between social classes. Migration from the countryside to the city increased dramatically because of the expansion of education and new development projects, as well as the growth of government bureaucracy, the public sector, and the army. Likewise, government activity in the countryside increased and along with it the number of government officials sent there from the capital. The result was a mingling of the various walks of life in a manner unfamiliar before the revolution. One result of this was that some segments of the lower class (or that had been until recently of the lower class) and residents of the countryside and provincial cities began to wear European clothing, while the banning of the tarboosh and the increased wearing of shoes resulting from the rise in income further weakened the role of dress in class distinction. Other bases for distinction, such as the location of residence, mode of transportation, manner of speech, and means of entertainment, began to disappear. And so did the differences in the nature of religious discourse, which I will take up again in another chapter.

Provincial cities grew quickly with the rapid growth of the middle class in the countryside; so, too, did new neighborhoods sprout up on the edges of already existing suburbs of large cities to accommodate the new entrants to the middle class coming from within or without these cities. Some such existing neighborhoods spread out into the desert and encroached upon surrounding agricultural lands. For example, the villages and agricultural plots of land near the Pyramids area turned into middle-class residential neighborhoods. Some described this spreading of the middle class as the 'ruralization of the cities' or alternatively, the 'urbanization of the countryside.' Whichever it was, it is certain that throughout the 1950s and 1960s the middle-class grip on manners associated with 'urbanity' lessened, and members of this class became much less distinguishable from the inhabitants of the countryside and the lower classes in the cities than they had ever been.

It was only natural that the up-and-coming lower classes would not remain confined to their old neighborhoods, but betook themselves to the old neighborhoods of the middle classes with their parks, leisure clubs, and beaches. The pre-revolutionary era promenades in downtown Cairo, with their restaurants, cafés, theaters, and cinemas hitherto used exclusively by the middle class, had, by the late 1960s, been invaded by these rising sections of the lower classes. Distinguishing them from the old middle class now required a look at their facial features, which could betray their rural origins, or to observe their manner and tone of speech, or way of gesturing and laughing.

They also invaded the venerable leisure clubs (called 'sports clubs'). These had in the pre-revolutionary era been restricted to the use of foreigners and members of the Egyptian upper class, in addition to a small segment of the upper middle class. This exclusivity, however, was deemed contrary to the maxims of the revolution, and soon more and more people who had never had access to these clubs acquired both the taste and the ability to get past their doors. The same may be said for the beaches of Alexandria, as well as the universities and foreign private schools, which after the revolution came to be referred to as 'language schools.'

All of this inevitably led to a greater mobility between neighborhoods in the large cities and between the smaller and larger cities, which created unanticipated pressure on the public transportation system. This created a real problem that had not existed before the revolution, requiring a solution similar to the need for new housing, new schools, and new water and sewer utilities.

An interesting change came over Egyptian trains as well as their passengers. While the type of first-class passenger changed with the change of the nature of social elites from rich landowners and cabinet ministers to army officers and the new officials of the public sector, the demand for second-class cars increased much more than that for third-class cars, meaning the conditions of the second class were bound to deteriorate. Meanwhile, the state of the third-class cars improved somewhat. These changes were a reflection of what happened to the three social classes: a radical change in the upper class, a rapid growth in and deterioration of the middle class, and a rise in status of the lowest.

Education continued to be the principal means available to the lower classes of rising into the middle class, but the extraordinary expansion of education in the 1950s and 1960s was associated with a big drop in its quality; a result of the overcrowding of schools on the one hand and the decline in the quality of teaching on the other. It is difficult to separate this decline in education from the decline in quality of the written language, the increase in the use of colloquialisms in writing, and the beginnings of the 'dumbing down' of different forms of cultural production: journalism, broadcasting, original and translated literature, as well as university textbooks.

All this led the Egyptian middle class to lose more of its distinctive features during the first two decades after the revolution. It was no longer that old urbane class, with its fine education, distinctive dress, and residential areas, which took pride in its skill and proficiency in eloquent Arabic writing. Did the new middle class also lose part of that strong patriotic sentiment of the pre-revolutionary middle class?

Whoever tries to judge the strength of the sense of patriotism prevailing in the 1950s and 1960s from the writings of such prominent journalists as Ahmad Bahaa al-Din or Salah Hafez, of writers and playwrights such as Yusuf Idris and Nu'man Ashur, poets like Salah 'Abd al-Sabur and Ahmad Higazi, or songs written by Salah Jahin and sung by 'Abd al-Halim Hafez with the beautiful new music written for them by Kamal al-Tawil, Muhammad al-Mogi, or Baligh Hamdi, must reach the conclusion that the sense of patriotism was definitely stronger then than it had been before the revolution. But there is no doubt that the degree of opportunism also increased among some of the ranks of the middle class during the same period.

Again, no one can deny the elevated level of cultural production of the middle class in those two decades, effectively promoting the slogans of the revolution and engendering optimism in the various arenas of culture. The number of published original and translated books increased greatly, while the General Book Organization, which was established by the state, was noticeably active in publishing new books and re-releasing old titles from the country's literary heritage. The number of newspapers and radio and television stations increased at the start of the 1960s. So, too, did the number of theaters and cinemas. A new space was created for folk arts and for ballet, music, and song, all expressing the spirit of the new revolution and meeting the need of the middle class for new ways of expression. Faster, and more optimistic, music and songs expressed the optimism and joy of the new middle class at its new social ascent and the higher degree of emancipation for women as a result of the opening of the door to their education and employment.

In the social and economic arenas, the middle class carried out, with energy and competence, what was requested of it by the revolutionary government: in public sector administration, in the management of the Suez Canal after its nationalization, and in various social and cultural services that the revolution had expanded and spread throughout Egypt, whereas, beforehand, such services had been limited to the large cities. To be sure, some of these services, such as education, became impaired and declined in quality, but this was the result of the greater enthusiasm for greater quantity, even if at the expense of quality.

The middle class in the 1950s and 1960s was not flawed by weak patriotism or low energy but by government impositions upon it. Cultural production and economic growth proceeded according to the orders of the state; intellectuals and those who worked in the areas of economic and social development were governed by the wishes of the state and merely executed its plans. This flaw did not appear too serious as long as the sentiments of the intellectuals and those who implemented economic policy were congruent with the direction of the state. I remember, during this time, when Nasser announced the ten-year plan (1959/60–1969/70) for social and economic development, the view of most economists was that the goal of doubling the national income in ten years was overly ambitious and almost impossible to realize after a nearly fifty-year period of stagnation in per capita income. When they expressed their doubts to Nasser, he said, "Just tell me how much money you need to implement the investments of the plan, and I guarantee I'll get it for you." He meant that through his foreign policy he could obtain the necessary economic aid from both east and west without needing to reduce greatly the people's already low level of consumption. The government by itself would undertake the whole burden, and nothing would be demanded of the people except obedience. As for culture, creativity and initiative were, of course, needed, but without anybody crossing the line drawn by the state.

The platitudes continued throughout the honeymoon that occurred between government and the people, but a split started to appear at the beginning of the 1960s with the dissolution of the union between Syria and Egypt, and Egypt's dispatching troops to Yemen. As the fear of being overthrown began to overtake the regime, it tightened its grip on personal freedom, gradually turning Egypt into a police state. The subjugation of both intellectuals and bureaucrats increased, patriotic fever subsided, creativity weakened, and productivity declined.

Such complete subjugation to the state was really what aroused feelings of resentment against the revolution from some prominent intellectuals, such as Naguib Mahfouz and Tawfiq al-Hakim, even if they could not express it openly. It also aroused resentment from some prominent Egyptian economists, who withdrew completely from public life, some of them emigrating abroad for many years.

It was not only true, as was said at the time, that the government was "implementing socialism without socialists," the government was also putting into effect an economic plan without economists, and a cultural plan without concerning itself much with the opinions of intellectuals. What was indeed amazing was that, in spite of all this, the government managed to achieve dazzling success for a while in terms of social and economic development, and a cultural renaissance of sorts. But it is also not surprising that, when the government was struck with a crushing military defeat in 1967, progress ceased in every sphere, and the state that had been directing everything disappeared.

In the twenty years following the defeat, the rapid growth of the Egyptian middle class continued, indeed at a much faster rate than it had in the fifteen years following the revolution, as the middle class absorbed additional broad segments of the lower classes. So, too, did the middle class continue to lose even more of the features that had distinguished it in the monarchical era. During the Sadat era there was also a decline in the intensity of patriotic fervor and a decrease in the level of productivity in both the cultural and economic fields.

3

When chronicling the history of an entire century, some historians note that the true beginning may not be the first year of the century, and the true end may not be its last. So they may write about, say, the 'short twentieth century' or the 'long nineteenth century' on the basis, for example, that what really distinguishes the twentieth century happened between the beginning of the First World War in 1914 and the fall of the Berlin Wall in 1989, which is a period shorter than one hundred years. They may also consider that what truly distinguishes the nineteenth century are the events that took place between the French Revolution in 1789 and the beginning of the First World War, a period longer than one hundred years.

By that measure, we can say that what really distinguished the Sadat era from those before and after it with regard to the development of the Egyptian middle class did not start with Sadat's assumption of the presidency in 1970; rather it began with the inauguration of the *infitah* in 1974. Nor did it end with the assassination of Sadat in 1980, but rather with the ending of the golden age of migration of Egyptian labor to the Gulf in the mid-1980s. So, what exactly happened to the middle class in Egypt during this period, which is slightly longer than ten years?

Those were indeed the two most important factors affecting the development of the Egyptian middle class under Sadat: the launching of the Open Door policy and the increase in migration to the oil-rich countries of the Gulf and Libya. Those two events opened the floodgates of opportunity for social ascent, bringing a large number of the lower class into the middle class over a very short period of time and stamping the middle class with characteristics that it did not have before.

As we have already noted, this period (1974–86) witnessed a very high rate of economic growth (more than 8 percent). But the rapid growth was originating not in industry or agriculture, but mainly in services, including remittances from workers working abroad and the Suez Canal revenues, in addition to the rise of the price of oil. All of these sources of rapid income growth are sometimes referred to by economists as 'rentier' income; that is, income not derived from productive activity, and accruing with little sacrifice or effort. There is a clear difference between the income from such sources and the income from agriculture, or industry, or other services. The rate of inflation was bound to rise as a result of such a big increase in expenditure without a corresponding increase in production. Opportunities for making large gains were opened by inflation and migration, especially in that most Egyptian labor migrating to the Gulf was from low-income groups. All this, together with the continued expansion of education which had started in the two previous decades, and the opening of new universities in provincial towns, caused the middle class to grow very rapidly and to acquire other new characteristics which made it even more difficult to distinguish its members from other classes.

Things got into a muddle again, but this time to a much greater extent than they had under Nasser. Now the middle class, even more than in the Nasser era, became both urban and rural, educated and illiterate. Distinguishing the middle class by sight became harder than ever, as western clothing spread and new types of consumer goods became more common without their consumers becoming any more 'modern.' New segments of society also began going to the theaters, beaches, and entertainment outlets with which they had been unfamiliar until very recently, and it was only inevitable that the theaters and entertainment outlets would start responding to their taste.

Television also became very widespread during this period, further contributing to the obliteration of differences between the classes and to the difficulty in distinguishing one from the other. It was not merely that television entered all homes, but the programs it presented contributed to closing the gap by exhibiting to all the new style of life that everyone might lead. Some new consumer goods came within reach of almost everyone, such as tape recorders, transistor radios, and sunglasses, in addition to the services of hairdressers, while children's birthday celebrations on the lines of the old middle-class celebrations were adopted by the newcomers to this class.

It was also during this period that the phenomenon of veiling became widespread, that is, women covering their hair and wearing wide, long-sleeve dresses that fell all the way to the feet. Much has been said to explain this change in Egyptian women's dress that became noticeable in the mid-1970s, but, regardless of its explanation, the spread of the *higab* (veil) added to the difficulty in distinguishing the old middle class from the new, and likewise between the middle class as a whole and other segments of society with lower incomes.

It is obvious, then, that technological progress in manufacturing consumer goods, which took place in the industrialized countries, especially Japan, began to affect the ability to distinguish the middle class from others by making many goods available to people of lower income. More of these goods were now produced, and at various qualities and of varying prices, such that one brand could not easily be differentiated from another just by sight. The best example of this was blue jeans, which by then came in different types, but it was not easy to distinguish what was cheap from what was expensive.

Of course, this phenomenon did not apply only to Egypt, and not even to Third World countries alone; it appeared in the richer countries as well, so that if we add other developments, such as wider access to education, the appearance of the welfare state, and long periods of full employment we may understand what a British politician meant when he said, "We are all middle class now." This is, of course, an exaggeration, but it touches on an important truth, which means, in the case of Egypt, that ten years after the *infitah* and massive migration to the Gulf, the middle class had become much bigger than it had ever been, in absolute terms as well as relative to the total population, and it became harder than at any other time before to distinguish it from other classes.

By the mid-1980s the sense of patriotism and enthusiasm for any national issue also became weaker. What is more, the quality of achievements of the middle class in the cultural and economic fields has also declined compared to its contributions during the 1950s and 1960s.

It may be sufficient to note what happened during the 1970s to the most prominent artists and intellectuals of the 1950s and 1960s: their increasing frustration, their decline in status, and sometimes even their complete disappearance from the scene—without being replaced by a new generation able to match their level of creative activity. In the economic field, the Egyptian middle class was weakened in the pre-revolution years by foreign dominance over the Egyptian economy, and in the 1950s and 1960s by being completely subjected to the wishes and directives of the state. By the 1970s it had become subject neither to a foreign occupier nor to an oppressive state, but to feverish consumption which brought great damage both to intellectual life and to economic productivity, in addition to its negative impact on patriotism. In the 1970s we thought we were seeing the worst in the three spheres, but it later appeared that things could become even worse.

4

During the following three decades (1980–2010), the Egyptian middle class suffered a series of blows that slowed its growth rate sharply, lowered its standard of living, and made it even less distinguishable from the lower class. It was inevitable that this would be reflected in a further weakening of its patriotic sentiment as well as in a lower ability to participate in political, economic, and cultural life.

The first blow came, as we have already seen, with the sharp drop in oil prices in 1986, which dried up one of the important wellsprings of growth for the middle class: migration to the Gulf. The concomitant reduction in oil exports of the Gulf states led to their reduced demand for Egyptian labor while the reduction of Egyptian oil exports led to reduced public spending, harming large segments of the middle class.

With the advent of the 1990s, the harm increased from two sides: 1) Saddam Hussein's attack on Kuwait, which compelled many Egyptian émigrés in the Gulf to return to Egypt; and 2) the Egyptian government's signing of an agreement with the International Monetary Fund in 1991 which led to further reductions in public spending.

We have already seen how these two developments were combined with a large increase in the unemployment rate, which led to a decreased rate of mobility from the lower class to the middle class, as well as to a lowering of the standards of living of both classes. It is true that education continued to provide the opportunity for low-income earners to move into the middle class, but that opportunity gradually faded with the spread of unemployment among the ranks of graduates of university, colleges, and higher institutes.

The inflation rate, though lower than it had been during the Sadat era, was high enough to cause a noticeable decline in the middle-class standard of living, especially with a large reduction in government subsidies given to several essential goods and services. Another factor that brought the Egyptian middle class nearer to the lower classes was that the prices of some durable goods, such as refrigerators, washing machines, televisions, tape players, and telephones did not rise as high as the general rate of inflation, which made such goods more available to the masses. The quality of education received by the children of the middle class did not differ very much from that received by poorer children, even though the poor were less able to pay the exorbitant fees demanded for private tuition. The large rise in the cost of accommodation also reduced the distinction derived from quality or place of residence. Electricity and piped-in water had reached almost everyone, even if the available drinking water was becoming of doubtful quality for drinking. Large swaths of the middle class, like the class below it, had become unable to afford buying purified bottled water. Television had, more than ever, become a means of mass entertainment, the landline telephone became a fixture in every house, and the mobile telephone came to be seen in the hands of many people of every class. The cafés, restaurants, and beaches that used to accept only members of the middle class now opened their doors to everyone, but their quality had in any case declined to such an extent that they could hardly be distinguished from the coffee shops, restaurants, and beaches that the lower class would frequent.

This weakening of various features that used to distinguish the Egyptian middle class has caused many to speak of the 'disappearance of the middle class in Egypt,' and the eminent Egyptian economist Dr. Ramzi Zaki to write a book in the early 1990s titled *Wida'an li-l-tabaqa al-wusta* (Farewell to the Middle Class). What has happened may indeed be a kind of disappearance, which may justify using the expression 'farewell'; but it is not exactly extinction as much as being 'lost in the crowd.' One may now walk in the streets, ride the various means of mass transit, frequent different coffee shops, restaurants, and beaches, stroll through university campuses, watch children leaving school, and young men and women promenading along the Corniche, and probably not see anyone other than members of the middle class, not one of them bearing any class distinction from the rest. Admittedly, one may see some poor, worn-out street vendor or an emaciated lowly policeman ready to do anything you ask him for a small tip. With the exception of those, and with the addition of poor agricultural workers, there does not seem to be any other than a 'middle class.' A whole class seems to have disappeared, or dissolved into another, to form a single large mass of people, all looking the same and having the same hopes.

Something similar happened to Egyptian trains. A large number of passengers have crept out of third-class carriages and crammed into the second class, which is no longer any better than the third class. But second-class passengers cannot afford a more comfortable mode of conveyance, so they have to be content where they are. Some of them do filter into the first class, but the first class has itself declined in comfort, because there is no longer a passenger among all three classes that can bear the costs it would take to travel with a reasonable amount of comfort and cleanliness. It is as if the entire train has come to consist of a single class of carriage, even though the Railroad Authority still considers there to be three.

But where did the upper class go? The answer is that, of course, the upper class still exists; indeed its numbers must have greatly increased since the monarchical (semi-feudal) era; and they have certainly increased far beyond their number in Nasser's socialist era, and beyond that of Sadat's (infitah) era. Hence, neither feudalism nor socialism and not even Sadat's Open Door policy managed to generate as great a number of rich people as the Mubarak era has. Great wealth has been generated in this latest era, not by large agricultural land holdings, the occupation of high office in a socialist state, or the import/export trade; more important than all of that has been the marriage of money and power.

This new upper class enjoys its wealth farther from view than the upper classes of any earlier era had. This is not only because it has acquired much of its wealth in violation of the law, but also because the divide between the type of life led by the upper class and that of the classes below it exceeds any difference that existed between classes in all of Egypt's modern history.

The members of this class do not go about the streets as we do, nor are they to be seen in the types of restaurants, clubs, or beaches that we may frequent, and they do not usually ride trains, as we do. We may see some of their pictures in the newspapers, and read news about some of their weddings, but no more than that. This is because they live in places where they have their own private clubs and beaches; they travel in airplanes or in automobiles with tinted windows, impossible to see into. Their houses are kept secure by strict guards, who allow no one to approach them, for, if one were to approach, one might discover a lifestyle completely unknown to Egyptians.

Nothing like this was present in the monarchical era. These new rich have benefited from sixty years of technological development in the production of consumer goods; goods that did not exist at all in the era of the monarchy, not in the era of Nasser, or of Sadat. The 'consumer society' had not yet arrived in the days of the king or those of Nasser. In the Sadat era it had just emerged. In the era of Mubarak, more than in any other era in modern Egyptian history, Egypt has come to be divided into 'two nations' living in one country. This begs the question: could it be that the threefold familiar classification of society into upper, middle, and lower classes has lost much of its usefulness?

One of the uses of this threefold classification is to draw attention to the class in the middle that has an amount of leisure and education not enjoyed by the lower class, and has aspirations different from those of both the upper and lower classes, and also a stronger feeling of patriotism because of these very aspirations. All this goes a long way toward explaining why the middle class tends to play a much more important role in its country's economic, political, and cultural development than that played by the other two classes. But to what use can such classification be put in view of the conditions that prevail in Egypt today, when the middle class shares with the lower class the same frustration, the same small amount of leisure, and almost the same low level of education?

7

The Intellectuals

1

If corruption has indeed spread so widely in Egypt's economic and political life, how could it have spared Egypt's intellectual life?

When one remembers or reads about the prevailing cultural climate in the monarchical era, it seems that there was nothing to prompt the spread of corruption among intellectuals the way there is today: not in the type of government of the day, not in the nature of the education they received, not in economic conditions, and not in the media.

The monarch sat at the summit of power, but, unlike the president of the republic in the new regime that arrived with the revolution of 1952, it was rare that he would interfere with the promotion or demotion of someone because of a personal relationship with that person or any enmity he may have felt toward them. This was not exactly because of the king's personal qualities, but because of the nature of the political system put in place by the constitution of 1923. True, it was within the power of the king to bestow the title of pasha or bey on whomever he pleased, but the title did not win any money for the one holding it. Indeed, even this granting of title was for a long time subject to checks and balances, a departure from which would have seemed shameful. Some of the literati might indeed have coveted a title and might compose a paean or speech extolling the king for the purpose of acquiring one, but this remained a very rare occurrence up to the last years of King Farouk, and in any case it did not do much harm to the public interest.

It was possible for the king to indicate his wish to favor some intellectual by having him appointed preferentially to some high position over someone else who may be more worthy of it, or to grant him some prize that he did not really deserve. But what may seem surprising now, after all we have seen in the following eras, is how often such favors were opposed and went unfulfilled.

The king, by constitutional writ, "reigned but did not govern," and with few exceptions this was the way things were. The true power to promote, award bonuses, demote, and fire lay in the hands of the prime minister and the cabinet. Moreover, many of those very same cabinet and prime ministers were themselves prominent intellectuals; quite the opposite of what we have seen later. And it is not surprising that well-educated[10] prime ministers and cabinet members tend to treat other intellectuals better than their counterparts who are not as well educated.

For example, in the pre-revolutionary era, those who took the office of minister of education were almost all men of letters. It is true that to be ready to engage in corrupt practices is not affected necessarily by a person's level of education, but there is no doubt that to be ready to corrupt, for example, the teaching faculties at universities and schools, or to order the teaching of certain books simply to profit the authors who may have some personal connection to the minister, is a less likely occurrence the higher the level of education of the minister or his deputies. One cannot imagine, for example, that one of those earlier ministers, or even a deputy in a ministry that they headed, would allow the publication of the types of readers and history books that we see today being issued by the Ministry of Education to be used as textbooks at government schools. Rather, one still remembers how, in the era of those ministers, the books assigned to students on Arabic language and literature included selections that were chosen and explained by the crème of the Egyptian intelligentsia, and which, before they were released into the hands of students, were reviewed by some of the pillars of Egyptian culture.

What was in the power of the rulers before the revolution to subvert the intelligentsia compared to what the post-revolutionary leaders became able to do? In those years an intellectual might possibly rise to become a minister, but he must also be a politician. It was not enough for an intellectual in the pre-revolution era to reach the office of minister merely by strengthening his ties to those in power or by writing a series of articles in praise of the king or prime minister. Usually, he had to be a member of a political party, and people would be quite surprised at the appointment of a minister with no political history and about whom they knew neither his political inclination nor proclivity, and whose name they had never heard beforehand, as frequently happens today.

Once, the prominent writer ‘Abbas al-‘Aqqad wrote an elegiac poem to King Farouk, and another equally prominent writer, Taha Hussein, while a minister of education, startled his audience with a phrase he uttered in a speech in the presence of the king at the inauguration of Farouk University in Alexandria, to wit: “your majesty has bestowed honor on knowledge.” However, such occurrences were so rare that people were inclined to search for hidden meanings behind them. Was al-‘Aqqad trying to protect himself from the wrath of the king because of an article he had written that was critical of him? Was Hussein motivated only by his desire to further his project of free education? Or was he simply, as he himself said in justification of his words, “describing the king not as he was but as he ought to be?”

In any case, the ministers of education of that era did not by any means shower money on those intellectuals close to them or on those whom the regime may have favored, granting them prizes for an allegedly great scholarly or artistic work that they might or might not have produced. Nor was there a state-run organization with a name like The General Egyptian Book Organization publishing books of dubious quality, merely because the authors were able to win the favor of state officials. Cultural works were produced almost exclusively by private publishers, and they did not receive any financial support from the state unless the state established that their work really deserved funding. Plays were mounted by private troupes and films produced by private production companies. High-brow newspapers and magazines were also released by private publishing houses that relied on the continued favor of their public. There were no such things as ‘national newspapers’ whose editors-in-chief were appointed by the government according to whim, regardless of talent, with the literati (or illiterati) competing to gain appointment as editors or columnists by writing what pleased the government.

The economic and social pressure that might push an intellectual to sacrifice his integrity for the sake of material gain was also very weak in the pre-revolutionary era. The low inflation rate and the slow pace of social mobility before 1952 were two factors limiting the spread of corruption among the intelligentsia as well as among others. I have said above, when discussing the development of the middle class, that the great majority of its members during the first half of the twentieth century had risen from humble origins mainly through education. Such upward social mobility is a slow process, as opposed to ascending by means of profits from commerce or industry, by migration to an oil-producing state, or through proximity to political power, as Egypt was to witness later. But someone who rises slowly in material and social status by means of education is probably less willing to submit to the allure of money or to sacrifice principle for personal gain than is someone who has tasted sudden wealth and high living standards for reasons that have little to do with education or effort. One is therefore inclined to maintain that the nature of upward mobility realized by the Egyptian intelligentsia during the first half of the twentieth century was among the reasons why they were less willing to engage in corruption than were their counterparts in the second half of the century. They gained their status by effort and sacrifice and not by cunning, and in an environment in which effort and education were able to bring them more benefit than cunning ever could. Along those lines, the intelligentsia hoped for nothing more than people's approval as a reward for their efforts, and they gained it. But when rewards became dissociated from merit, they shifted to other kinds of work. Some of them succeeded, and some of them failed, but it became clear that a completely new climate had emerged in which Egyptian intellectuals started to play a dismal role. This new climate originated with the 1952 revolution, but it became increasingly worse with the passing of time.

2

The 1952 revolution created a demand for a different type of intellectual from the type previously needed. For here was a group of revolutionary officers who had managed to eliminate the old political parties and remove them from the centers of power from which they had ruled Egypt since 1919. These were young officers with no prior political experience in holding office and hardly any knowledge of economic issues or foreign policy. They may have had glorious goals and seductive slogans; but how could they implement them without soliciting the aid of law specialists, diplomats, economists, engineers, and agriculturalists to translate the principles of the revolution into new legislation, new types of international relations, and new economic policies?

The need for a new breed of 'thinker' arose as well. The goals of the revolution were inevitably ill-defined and needed people who would make them clearer and, perhaps, even to provide some theoretical framework for them. Indeed, the leaders of the revolution needed someone to clarify to them what they themselves meant by these goals and explain the relationship that existed between their goals and the prevailing world ideologies.

Finally, they also needed propagandists. These may not necessarily have believed in the goals of the revolution, but they had to be well-spoken rhetoricians who could write rousing articles in the newspapers and give convincing speeches. All of these, then, were needed: technocrats, thinkers, and propagandists. The term uniting all of them may be 'intellectuals,' even if this involves some extension of the original meaning of the term. A thinker must surely be an intellectual, but not necessarily a diplomat, economist, or engineer. A propagandist may be an intellectual, but more often is not.

The important thing is that if the rulers before the revolution needed intellectuals of the first type (for how else were they to conduct the affairs of state?), they did not need thinkers or propagandists to any comparable degree to that which the leaders of the revolution needed them. Every party before the revolution did have its own newspaper, which defended it against its opponents, and even the king himself occasionally made use of intellectuals to defame some party members who opposed him. But what might the king do that could need hypocritical praise? Some writer or journalist might extol the youth of the king or exaggerate people's love for him on his jubilee, but all of this did relatively little harm and had little impact. Such instances of hypocrisy would recall the ancient Arab poets' insincere flattery of the ruler more than it would inspire anger or great contempt. Encomiums for party leaders were also rare and of little influence. As for the thinkers of the day, they hardly ever employed their talent in the service of one ruler or another. In any case, the policies followed before the revolution were not formed by beliefs and ideologies, rather they were defined by the British.

All this changed with the coming of the revolution. The new regime advocated new principles that required that people be convinced of them. There were unfamiliar laws and unprecedented measures that needed explanation and justification. Perhaps more important was that the new regime had taken power by force, without recourse to a parliament or elections, and had replaced party rule with the rule of one man, who wished to retain power for as long as possible. He had to find 'intellectuals' willing to help him fulfill this mission.

The mission seemed honorable enough in the first few years of the revolution, during which a number of factors protected the Egyptian intelligentsia from the fall that occurred later on. During those early years the new regime enjoyed general support from the people and a singular enthusiasm that enabled it to seek the aid of intellectuals of the highest integrity, who were willing to defend the revolution and justify its policies with complete conviction. But it was soon to become clear to the leaders of the revolution, as well as to these intellectuals, that what the new regime really needed was a different type of intellectual.

People did remain enthusiastic about the revolution until after the schism between Nasser and Muhammad Naguib, the first president of Egypt, even if it lost the revolution some of its supporters. Indeed, people's enthusiasm increased with the nationalization of the Suez Canal and the forming of a political union with Syria,[11] and the revolution acquired even more supporters with the nationalizations of 1961. Nevertheless it was these achievements themselves that strengthened the trend toward dictatorship by whetting the appetite of the ruler for more power. This must have led, in turn, to the growth of another type of intellectual anxious to curry favor with those in power. These soon grew more numerous, as they experienced the regime's favorable response.

But then Nasser suddenly took harsh measures against Egyptian communists and other leftists, among whom were some of the most prominent intellectuals and talented artists. For some reason Nasser seems to have preferred to nationalize companies, to implement income redistribution measures, and to ensure that workers got their fair due by involving them in management, all in the absence of socialists and communists. He put many of them in jail, and some were tortured. Those who managed to evade imprisonment did so only by fleeing the country. By the end of the 1950s and the beginning of the 1960s, there was bound to appear on the face of public life a kind of intellectual who professed faith in the principles of the regime without really believing in them. These were quite capable of giving speeches or writing books, and even songs, in praise of Arab socialism, positive neutrality, and Arab nationalism, and disparaging colonialism and foreign dominance, all for the sake of currying favor with power. Those in power must have known full well the nature and purpose of such 'intellectuals,' but they favored them all the same for one simple reason: they were men without principles and no political history, who could, therefore, be relied upon to do whatever was asked of them.

This type of intellectual could no doubt be found in any country, and certainly existed before as well as after the revolution, but there is also no doubt that the political climate prevailing in Egypt from the mid-1950s to the beginning of the 1960s encouraged their emergence in an explosion of activity and brought to light their hidden talents. Some of these were known by everyone to be opportunists, but the true mettle of many others remained undiscovered until the policies of the regime changed completely between the 1950s and 1960s. It became clear to everyone that they possessed qualities that were bound to please any ruler who happened to appear, and they did, indeed, remain close to power throughout the 1960s and 1970s.

It was during this period (1958–64) that many prominent intellectuals withdrew into semi-retirement. Seeing that the climate was not fitting to them, they refused to participate. It was, nevertheless, also a period in which new intellectual stars began to shine, individuals who were at one and the same time talented and also sympathetic to the regime. Joining them, after their release from prison in 1964, was a large group of Marxist intellectuals, who were now given important responsible jobs in publishing organizations and in the state management of the cinema and theater. But when the military defeat came in 1967 all of their lights were extinguished, new and old. Some fell into the silence of grief and despair, and some migrated to the Gulf or to Europe. Whoever continued to write did so with stifled enthusiasm or turned from writing brilliant fiction to writing valueless articles. Others turned from writing poetry to serving in administrative posts.

This period lasted about eight years (from 1967 until 1975), until Egypt entered the era of *intifah*, reconciliation with Israel, distancing herself from the Arabs, and building strong ties with the United States. This gave life to a revitalized cultural climate, but its vitality was tarnished by a great deal of corruption.

3

The transformation that came about in the Sadat era in economic and foreign policy, as well as in Egypt's policy toward other Arabs states, led Egyptian intellectuals to split into three camps. There were those who found their hopes fulfilled in opening up to the west and reconciliation with Israel. They had not sympathized with Nasser when he closed the door to western goods and culture, nor had they been sympathetic to his Palestinian policy, or his advocacy of Arab nationalism. Instead, they preferred that Egypt be left alone to see to its own affairs and to use its resources for the development of its economy. At the head of these were some of the intellectuals who had remained silent during the Nasser era or wrote allegorical stories or essays on other subjects. When Nasser died one of them wrote that during his era it were as if they had "lost consciousness," but now they had regained it. Some of them returned to penning for the theater after a long absence or helped Sadat in writing his memoirs, joining him in his long strolls, with Sadat finding pleasure in their company after spending many years in the shadow of Nasser.

These writers who supported Sadat were being hypocritical since they had said or written little in support of Nasser while he was alive, and when they did it was obvious that they did it out of fear of Nasser and not out of any love for him.

There was another group of intellectuals who did not deny their past and continued to defend Nasser's policies after his death. They locked with the Sadatists in violent dispute, permitted by Sadat as part of the new freedoms he granted. Thus, economists calling for the protection of national industries battled with those loyal to Sadat in heated discussions at annual conferences. Those opposed to reconciliation with Israel clashed with those raising the banner of peace and approving of Sadat's official visit to Jerusalem. Those believing in Arab nationalism attacked Sadat's new direction toward reducing ties with other Arab states and were angered by what seemed to be Sadat's complete surrender to the United States and his apparent willingness to grant all of its demands. Those groups did not renounce anything they had written during the Nasser era and did not retreat from their belief in the necessity of achieving economic and political independence, of championing the Palestinians' cause, and of joining the ranks of the rest of the Arabs.

There remained that third type of intellectual willing in any era to work for private gain. Some of these had existed under Nasser, but they grew in number under Sadat when they found greater opportunities for personal gain under the *infitah* than had previously existed.

Thus, for example, we came to see an old Marxist and enthusiastic Nasserist attempting to formulate a new theory of the 'Sadat school of political thought,' while during the Nasser era he had been the editor-in-chief of a monthly magazine espousing exactly the opposite point of view. Likewise, economists who had previously written books extolling Arab socialism now published articles in praise of the *infitah*. Or university professors who had been active members of the Youth Organization, founded by Nasser to inculcate the belief in Arab socialism among young Egyptians, offered their services to Sadat in defense of his policies. Whereas previously they had defended Palestinian rights, some of them, who were now surprised and confused by Sadat's 1977 visit to Jerusalem and his reconciliation with the Israelis to the point of his delivering a speech to the Knesset, wrote articles that could be understood to give contradictory meanings: that they backed the visit, or perhaps that they were against it. One such individual preferred writing an article counting ten merits of the visit and ten faults.

Still, a large segment of Egyptian intellectuals could not really believe that Egyptian policy could possibly be turned on its head in this manner, and they continued to defend Nasser's policies until Sadat threw them all into jail in 1981.

4

After a brief period of optimism at the beginning of the Mubarak era, many Egyptian intellectuals were stricken with a frustration that has increased in strength little by little over the last twenty years. The optimism was triggered by Sadat's disappearance from the scene, but there were many reasons for the frustration that followed.

With the passing of time, it became clear that Mubarak's policies would not differ significantly from those of Sadat, whether in respect of the economy or relations with the Arabs, the United States, or Israel. True, the language was calmer; gone were the severe tones of Sadat's style that had perhaps been appropriate to the launching of new policies. Everything marched along the same road, but without the shouting. The *infitah* was ongoing at even greater speed, but without any attempt at justification. The neglect of the public sector and its selling off was proceeding apace, but in silence. Relations with the Arabs became even weaker, but without name-calling. Subservience to the United States persisted, coupled with greater self-debasement, but without describing the relationship as 'friendship,' as Sadat was wont to do. As for Israel, its demands were being met, and important economic agreements were signed with her, but these were signed quickly and without much discussion, as if the government really wished that they were made in secret, and the relations between the two countries were stabilized without a visit to Jerusalem by the Egyptian president and trumpeted about by the media, as had occurred under Sadat. In a climate of such deep despair, more of those opportunist intellectuals came to prominence. They were, indeed, as despairing as anyone else about the political and economic future of Egypt, but they were far from being despairing when it came to the realization of their own personal ambitions.

8

The Press

When President Sadat announced in the mid-1970s that he would grant
freedom to form political parties in Egypt and that he would permit each
party to have its own newspaper, this of course caused great joy, even if that
joy was for many mixed with some doubt and reservation. For this man
announcing freedom of the press was not known, whether from his political
history or his personal inclinations, for his liberalism or tolerance of opposition views. The stories we had heard about his political history before the
revolution told of his participation in some assassination attempts, his Nazi
sympathies, and later about his taking severe measures against those opposing the revolution in its early days—even sentencing them to death. This
did not augur well for democracy and free expression.

We soon saw such doubts confirmed. Feeling the strength of the
opposition movement against him, Sadat uttered a startling expression
when he described his type of democracy as "democracy with fangs." That
was, indeed, a very strange thing to hear from a man who prided himself
on the freedoms he had just granted. At the time he was launching these
new freedoms, Sadat was embarking upon a grave change of course in economic policy and in foreign policy in Egypt's stand toward Israel, toward
the United States, and toward Arab nationalism. We were quite right in
suspecting that all this new talk of freedom of opinion was nothing more
than granting the right to anyone who wished to criticize former policies.

Freedom to disagree really meant the freedom to disagree with Nasser's policies and to abandon what he had stood for. We felt that Sadat might easily go back on his promises for freedom of the press and expression as soon as he felt the slightest fear for himself or his new course of action.

Such fears proved well placed, for in the last three years of his rule, when Sadat sensed that his economic and foreign policies had given rise to greater dissent than he had anticipated, he did go back on his promises of greater freedom. Thus, when in 1977 the people protested against the rise in price of some necessities, Sadat met them with a greater degree of violence than that used against the monarchy at the beginning of the revolution. And, again, when many prominent writers expressed their displeasure at what Sadat called his 'Initiative,' meaning his official visit to Jerusalem in November of the same year, and at his signing separate peace agreements with Israel in 1978 and 1979, Sadat reacted with even greater force, using the expression "to grind" to describe what he might do to those who opposed him. His reaction came to a head in September 1981 when he closed all opposition newspapers and threw hundreds of the intelligentsia of all different political stripes in prison.

Among the first things that President Mubarak did after his assumption of power at the end of 1981 was to return to the shuttered newspapers the right to publish again. The press enjoyed a honeymoon of freedom of expression, the likes of which it had not seen since the beginning of the revolution. Unfortunately, this did not last long; indeed, throughout the twenty-nine years that have passed since the opposition papers were allowed to appear again, both the official and the opposition papers have suffered a steep decline. To grasp the nature of this decline, let us recall the state of the press in 1982 or 1983 and compare it with its current state.

In those days, we would read wonderful articles by the prominent independent writers Fathi Radwan and Hilmi Murad, which would appear regularly in *al-Sha'b*, the organ of the Labor Party. Both were to write enormously affecting articles in a very even temper and dazzling clarity of style, their power arising not from the force of their language but from the strength of their forthright argumentation.

At the same time, *al-Ahali*, the mouthpiece of the Tagammu' (Marxist) Party, was publishing articles no less powerful or forthright. Phillip Gallab would write his superb column entitled "Push Pin" and Salah Eissa his sarcastic commentaries, endowed with candor, good humor, and apt choice of target, which always hit their mark. The back page of *al-Ahali* used to publish a compellingly readable daily column in a small box at the bottom of the page—small but of great effect—comparing the conditions of the little guy and the big shot, and at the top of the page were the startlingly clever cartoons of Bahgat Othman. The newspaper *al-Wafd* also enjoyed wide popularity in those days, especially its weekly issue containing biting critiques of important personages.

What may seem most surprising today is what the government papers used to publish then as compared to what they publish now. There were the daily column of Ahmad Bahaa al-Din and the weekly columns of Yusuf Idris, along with the less regular and more academic articles of Louis Awad. Meanwhile, people would rush to look at Salah Jahin's cartoons every morning to get his take on some important issue or another. So, too, was Salah Hafez writing a regular column in *Akhbar al-youm* in which he gave free reign to his journalistic talent and his piercing insight.

The weekly magazine *Rose al-Youssef* did not exhibit the same boldness at the beginning of the Mubarak era that it had before the revolution. Nor was its sister magazine *Sabah al-khayr* what it had been in the 1950s, when it truly deserved the legend written below its name "for young hearts and free minds." Nevertheless, the two magazines were still, in the early 1980s, addressing genuine issues occupying the minds of the people. Nor had the cartoons for which they were famous yet lost their humor and the aptness of the subjects they chose to address.

There were two other important things about the 'national' newspapers at the beginning of the Mubarak era. One relates to the headlines of the front page and the other to photographs of the president and the First Lady. Of course, news related to the president continued to occupy a prominent position in the national newspapers and in the media in general—as has been Egypt's way with its rulers for a long time—but I remember that the front-page headlines of the early 1980s were sometimes about international issues without reference to the president. Details of great events of the world, such as the outbreak of a war or a threat made by one nuclear power toward another, were correctly assumed to be of more interest to the average Egyptian reader than some minutiae of news about the president. As for the photographs, it became known that immediately after the assassination of President Sadat the office of the presidency issued orders completely prohibiting the publishing of photographs of the president's wife without express permission. People interpreted this to mean that the Mubarak administration felt that one of the reasons for people's discontent with the former president in his last years was the frequent publication of news and photographs of Jehan Sadat and her repeated involvement in semi-official activities.

Many are the changes that took place within the Egyptian press since that time, and many are the possible explanations. Some may maintain that the change was due to Egypt losing several icons of the golden era of Egyptian journalism over the following two decades through the simple fact of death. But this is not a sufficient explanation since for every one of those great writers who has died one can name other talented writers who are still alive, active, and at the peak of their mental powers, but who are for some reason or another prevented from publicly expressing their views.

The transformation occurred step by step, until we arrived at a denuded journalistic desert that is very vast, it is true, for there are many more newspapers and magazines published today than there were twenty-five years ago. They are also much more technically advanced, but lack taste and influence. A new type of newspaper and magazine that did not exist in the 1980s has also joined the ranks, employing writers from every ideological stripe; such that what one column may say is robbed of its effectiveness by the column right next to it on the same page. But the quality of the printing, the fine production, and the high overheads compared to the low price per issue all give the impression that these publications are getting their funding from suspect quarters; and it is not always easy to know where those quarters are.

The papers that are still called 'national papers,' to differentiate them from the opposition papers, were struck by a number of maladies they had not previously suffered from. The editors-in-chief would now ask of the writers to distance their writing from anything that might arouse dangerous feelings in the readers on one hand or the anger of high officials on the other. The result has been a proliferation of stories and opinion pieces that do not say anything at all, or address issues with hardly any connection to what is occupying people's minds. Another malady that has struck so-called national newspapers is their insufferable ponderousness. This is closely tied to the former ailment, for apparently one of the hardest things for a writer to do is maintain some good humor while writing about subjects of no interest to readers or possibly to the writer himself.

In retrospect there was an endless array of means that the government might have used to arrive at this result, and indeed it has used them all. One of these has been to control the type of advertising that can appear in the opposition press and to control distributors. The government's monopoly over the few distribution networks available to the opposition press has enabled it to limit the number of copies placed on the street for sale at newsstands. It is stingy with the number of copies it provides to major sellers, while it piles them on to secondary sellers in remote outlets. It is the government that decides whether the papers will arrive in the provincial towns in the morning or the evening, or even whether they will arrive at all. Thus the government can easily control how many copies will remain unsold and returned to the publisher, and they may be in the tens of thousands, while many potential readers are trying in vain to find copies.

Aside from controlling distribution, and aside from the sword held over the heads of editors-in-chief of government magazines and newspapers who served yearly contracts and could be removed at the end of a term by a decision from the High Council of Journalism, there was also the means of offering temptation. The heads of opposition newspapers could be enticed with offers to install them in a government post provided that the offer was generous enough or at least proportionate to the degree of importance of the opposition paper. For some editors-in-chief it was enough to tempt them with positions as regular writers at important national papers, or even to offer them repeated invitations to appear on television; for others, nothing less than a seat in the upper house of parliament, or the position of a head of a brand new newspaper was sufficient. It was also helpful to keep loyal journalists happy and to guarantee their continuous co-operation with a liberal dispensation of privileges and displays of commendation, even for those whose loyalty is not in question. Hence, an annual prize was, and continues to be, awarded to prominent journalists and the heads of journalist associations supposedly for their distinguished intellectual and cultural contributions even though everyone knows how modest these contributions have been.

What is indeed striking is that, in spite of all these means at its disposal, the government has not succeeded in silencing everyone. There remain some stubborn journalists determined to stick to the principles they learned in their youths. In their case, the government has no recourse but to close down their newspapers entirely, or to imprison the journalist or editor-in-chief or both, and to haul them into court with the flimsy excuse of slander or the charge of "harming Egypt's reputation."

Even so, the government seems to have indeed achieved its goal, which is the near complete taming of the opposition. But there has been a price paid for it. The inevitable outcome has been that many readers abstained from reading the magazines and newspapers, and circulation dropped sharply. Editors-in-chief have tried to ignore the real reason for the decline, explaining it by the increased cost of living, while there are sufficient indications that the reason for many people's quitting the newspapers and magazines is not that the product now has a higher price, but that it has rotted.

In any case, the responsible parties at these newspapers have tried to avoid the problem and to keep bankruptcy at bay by resorting to the fastest and easiest solution. Having found it hard to attract readers interested in political debates because what attracts such readers does not meet with government approval, editors-in-chief have resorted to sport and sex. A surprising and unfortunate development has come over political cartoons, too. After the death or retirement of the giants of political cartooning of earlier decades, whose drawings and few words were often more powerful than long articles and commentaries, cartoonists have now found themselves in a lamentable position. Almost every subject has become forbidden, with every upper-level employee of the paper having the power to censor. And, with hope for reform so remote, it was hardly the time for irony and sarcasm. What is more, state officials began using the charge of defamation, sending editors and editors-in-chief as well as the cartoonists themselves to prison for long terms. The solution has been for cartoonists to resort to addressing very old subjects in a desperate attempt to inspire some laughter or a smile. They have gone back to topics like the relationship between the mother-in-law and her daughter's husband or the fat ugly wife beating and berating her frail husband when he comes home late, bringing to mind cartoons from the 1940s that appeared in a gloomy political climate bearing some similarity to ours.

Getting out of this predicament was especially difficult for some of the opposition newspapers. If the government papers managed to solve their own circulation problem by relying on sports news and sex, this path, if taken by the opposition papers, would be scandalous and the object of endless derision. For how could an opposition paper transform itself into a venue for provocative sexual stories, sports news, crime reports, or a TV guide? This might be acceptable in a 'national' newspaper, but how could it be so with an opposition paper?

Soon, opposition papers made a brilliant discovery: that they could solve the problem of declining readership by exploiting the dispute between secularists and Islamists, and even trying to inflame it. Thus we saw one opposition newspaper that had once been concerned with the class struggle finding the way out of its predicament, especially after the fall of the Soviet Union and the collapse of socialism, by stirring up an artificial battle between secularists and Islamists, which presented the paper with an inexhaustible source of publishable material. They even invented a new expression, 'Islamicize,' and its derivations, to describe the adversaries of secularism. On the other side, the pro-religious branch of the opposition press resorted to using the same debate as an alternative to confronting more urgent problems, accusing their opponents of being infidels. Thus the two found in the conflict between secularism and fundamentalism an easy way to rile the people without arousing the ire of the government. The government did not mind this at all, welcoming the fight as an excellent way to distract people's attention from what it was doing in other more pressing areas—normalizing relations with Israel and submitting to U.S. will—the latter dictated complete passivity toward repeated aggression against Iraq, Sudan, or Libya. The secularist–Islamic divide was, moreover, useful in distracting people from issues like election rigging, the spread of corruption, and widening income disparities. In fact, the government also found it useful to adopt changing positions in the dispute between the secularists and Islamists, now siding with one of them, now siding with the other. It would look the other way when some published novel or another used insulting language toward religion in the name of free expression and artistic license, and then impound others for doing the same thing while all of these novels were published by the same government-owned publishing house, with the government's full knowledge.

Meanwhile, we would from time to time hear of the imminent appearance of a new newspaper or magazine whose owners promised that their publication would make up for such deficiencies in Egyptian journalism, and we would anxiously await its arrival in the hope that someone would throw a stone into the stagnant pond. In most cases our hopes would be dashed. The outstanding exception was a daily paper called *al-Dustur*.

This was published by a talented group of young writers, enamored of journalism and not lacking in a sense of responsibility. The funding came from a private individual without any pretentions that his goal was to reform society or defend the nationalist cause. Even so, the newspaper took up every important issue, from normalization with Israel to income inequality, to corruption, to private foreign investment, to subjugation to American will, to the destructive effects of the media and pop culture, and so on. It did not consider any subject to be taboo except the call to normalize relations with Israel. Nor did it consider any organization off limits, be it governmental, financial, religious, or cultural. It did all of this at a high level of journalistic art and affability, something that readers had been missing for a long time. After just one or two issues of *al-Dustur* were published people began to ask themselves, "Had we really been deprived to such an extent from real journalism? Are we really now holding a paper whose headlines do not carry news of the president? Is it really true that a newspaper can tell the truth, but with good humor, and express what is really on people's minds, and that all that was needed was for the government to take its hand off the press and to leave it to manage its own affairs?" All that was indeed true and people snapped the paper off the stands, and its circulation continued to rise. A day's edition would sell out a few hours after it appeared, even though it was the only Egyptian newspaper in those days (the mid-1990s) that cost a whole Egyptian pound. Things kept up this way until the government decided that the situation was quite intolerable, so it concocted a crisis and shut it down.

In this barren desert, the government left nothing still pulsing or breathing with life except for one or two papers that it felt it could tolerate, at least for a while. Then in 2005 something happened marking a frightening development in the way the government treated opposition journalists. The situation had by then gone beyond denying the permission to publish, depriving the paper from advertising revenues, and controlling distribution; it had now come down to dealing blows. On 1 November 2005, the editor-in-chief of one opposition newspaper, about fifty years of age, slightly built, and frail of form, was walking home, for he did not own a car, in the early hours of the morning after spending a Ramadan night with friends and returning to his house in the Pyramids neighborhood where his wife and son were waiting for him. Allegedly, a car blocked his way and five big men he did not know got out, but they certainly knew him. They forced him into their car, gagging him so that he could not call for help, and blindfolding him so that he could not see their faces. They sped off to the other side of Cairo, all the while beating him on various parts of his body; his left eye began to bleed badly while the assailants repeatedly slashed him with sharp knives in the back of his neck and other parts of his body. This went on for about an hour and a half, with the poor man wondering whether it would end in his death. The whole time this was happening, his abductors were hurling awful insults at him until, upon reaching a spot on the Cairo–Suez road, they stripped him of his clothes, took his glasses, and threw him out into the desert in the dark of night, naked and shivering from the cold.

9

Religious Discourse

1

Over the course of its long history, extending more than a thousand years, al-Azhar, with its mosque and university, has been regarded by Egyptians as a religious symbol but also as a national one. It has remained since its founding (in AD 960) a bastion of Islam and of the Arabic language, and it has been in many periods of its history also a bastion of Egyptian nationalism. Despite all the hardships it has faced during the last one hundred years, al-Azhar has continued to graduate some of the most distinguished of Egyptian thinkers, such as Muhammad Abduh and Taha Hussein, who studied in al-Azhar and then revolted against it. They criticized its prolonged stagnation and its spirit of apathy, but they channeled the knowledge and expertise they had gained during their time in that very same institution to shake up the indifference and apathy in Egyptian social and cultural life.

It might be said that such critical Azharite thinkers are simply radical by nature, and as such would represent only a very small proportion of Azharites. The overwhelming majority have always been conservative, not bold enough to challenge the old and with no enthusiasm for the new. But the weakness of which I will speak now is not merely that of conservatism, sticking doggedly to the inherited traditions and rejecting anything new; for what has struck al-Azhar during the past two decades is a new malaise that is almost the exact opposite of conservatism.

The facts are that the Grand Sheikh of al-Azhar, the highest religious authority in Egypt (and one of the highest in the Islamic world), has indeed been more active than usual and has shown an unfamiliar readiness to pronounce his views on political issues, including expressing his complete support for this or that trend in foreign policy. Most of the time his activities have not been of the kind that one might expect from a bastion of Islam and of the Arabic language; so, too, have they been contrary to the direction adopted by the Egyptian nationalist movement.

We have long criticized al-Azhar for its hidebound opposition to any attempts at introducing some necessary and desirable changes, but we have come to be apprehensive about its unjustified rush to defend many changes that are neither necessary nor desirable. When an advocated reform was like a clean refreshing breeze with the aim of revitalizing the people and sparking a renaissance, we would be wary of al-Azhar's determination to oppose it. Now, however, when the new is more like a hurricane threatening to pull us up by the roots, we unfortunately see al-Azhar throwing open one door after another to let in this ill wind. To give just one example, in an attempt to goad people into casting their ballots in the referendum of the summer of 2005 to amend the constitution according to the government's wishes, the Sheikh of al-Azhar cited a verse from the Qur'an forbidding people from withholding their testimony, describing one who does so as having sinned. Refusing to participate in a referendum designed by a wicked government was thus considered the same as giving a false testimony before a judge.

2

I had two sisters much older than I, the elder born in 1919 and the younger two years later. I did not see either one of them at any stage of their lives, and until their death, ever wearing a covering of any kind on her hair, whether inside the home or outside of it. My father, Ahmad Amin, who was known for his books on Islamic history, never thought that he might be committing any sin by allowing his daughters to go out in public unveiled, even though he insisted throughout his life that women were obliged to dress with all due modesty.

My father was by no means exceptional in this regard. This was the attitude of the overwhelming majority of Egyptian middle-class families at the time, and it remained so until the mid-1960s, twenty years after my father died. Women in the Egyptian countryside had always covered their hair, and the urban middle class would insist that the poor country girls that came to serve in their houses do the same. They suspected a serving girl who left her hair uncovered to be a girl of loose behavior, and the lady of the house would scold her until she covered her hair. Covering the hair was thus obligatory for the serving women but not for the women they served. The issue, then, was purely one of class distinction and was rarely given a religious justification.

Religion indeed played a very small role in the life of my generation compared to the role it plays now. There was so little talk about religion, it was so rare for anyone to request an official religious opinion *(fatwa)* on some kind of behavior or another, and the amount of airtime and column space occupied by discussions of religious topics were far less than now, to say nothing of the amount of space such topics took up in school text-books. All of this was completely in keeping with people's attitudes about women covering their hair, about men displaying the 'raisin' on their foreheads, or about men growing beards.

For this reason, I felt very uncomfortable about calling what was happening in Egypt from the mid-1970s onward a 'religious awakening.' For religion had not been missing so that it might be rediscovered. What was happening was closer to being a 'reinterpretation of religion,' the new interpretation being much more extremist. This extremism has taken many forms, wearing a *higab* on the hair and around the face being one form, and insistence on covering the face itself being another. Yet another was the increased use of microphones to broadcast the call to prayer and other religious observances at all hours of the day, as well as the increase in the voluntary issuing of *fatwa*s on religious issues.

All this seems to go far beyond a 'religious awakening,' especially when it comes to wearing the face veil *(niqab)* instead of the *higab*, for it looks like a step toward a complete withdrawal from life or as if the woman so dressed is announcing at the top of her voice her denunciation of people who do not interpret religion as she does. Worse, still, is veiling children and young girls, depriving young children of some source of enjoyment of life, and dragging into children's minds thoughts that would not have occurred to them otherwise. This seemed to me not dissimilar to the fashion of introducing sex education for children in western schools, on the ground that it protects them from sexual assault by relatives and strangers.

As for the large number of women who do not wear the *higab*, either because they were raised in an environment similar to my own or because they had been born into a different faith, one can easily imagine their feeling of alienation in the midst of large numbers of veiled women. These could be their friends, who may have no feeling for them other than love and respect, but behind them is a long line of men and women who suggest by their actions or say outright that veiling is one of the conditions of being virtuous and of correct religious practice. It is also easy to imagine the contribution made by all this to increasing the gulf between Muslims and Copts.

Some say that behind this spread of religiosity is the adoption of customs and traditions widely popular in the Arab oil states and transported to Egypt by migrant workers. I am not inclined to accept such an explanation. Customs and patterns of behavior do not transfer with such ease, and they do not transfer at all unless the receiving country has prepared the ground for their acceptance and spread. Similarly, for one interpretation of religion to replace another, as happened with this extremist interpretation of Islam replacing a more moderate and tolerant one, is not a conceptual phenomenon but a social one. It does not happen because of people coming to believe in something of which they had not before been convinced, or their discovery of a true meaning of Qur'anic verses that had not previously been known to them. Rather, it happens because of a change that occurs in their feelings, their fears, and aspirations; a change which is attributable in turn to the shift that has occurred in their social conditions. Such a trend did happen in Egypt— and dramatically so—starting from the mid-1970s because of the *infitah*, labor migration, the change in economic policy, the rise in social mobility, and so on. All of this must be behind the transformation of people's interpretation of Islam, including the change in the attitude of men and women toward women wearing the veil.

There was nothing in this that could be called 'religious awakening,' nor can I see in it an 'intellectual or social retrogression.' The head covering that the great majority of the women of Egypt now wear is very different from the old head covering that village women still wear. Nor is it the same as the 'head kerchief' that urban lower-class women of the past century used to wear. Nor, yet, is it the head covering that women of the Egyptian middle class wore before the 1930s. Each of these different types of *higab* served a social and class-based function, and the *higab* widespread in Egyptian cities today also performs a special function which responds to the prevalent social conditions in Egypt. This may be confirmed by noting the development of Egyptian women's dress in the last ten years, wherein a growing number of Egyptian younger women, with their heads duly covered, have started wearing pants that might be loose or tight, and blouses or sweaters that may reveal more of the wearer's charms than they cover. One sees, today, Egyptian girls dressed in such a manner promenading along the Nile Corniche, hand in hand with young men who do not give the impression that they are these girls' husbands or fiancés. Some new social change must have occurred to require the *higab* to perform a different role from that which it played in the previous twenty years.

It follows from this that the wearing of the *higab* cannot be easily considered as 'retrograde' or that it represents a deterioration of the status of women. Indeed, its spread could be easily regarded as a new step along the road to the greater liberation of women. The spread of the *higab* may have something to do with Egyptian women having to leave the house to work, to study, or to bear burdens that their husbands once did before they migrated to the Gulf or before the onslaught of high rates of inflation. Women, therefore, now have to mix more with unrelated men in the streets, in universities, and in mass transit than they did before. Leaving the house wearing a *higab* may indeed be a step toward greater emancipation as compared to remaining bound to the home, with or without a veil.

3

In May of 2006, we heard of two startling religions *fatwa*s on two really bizarre issues. The *fatwa*s were issued by two high-ranking sheikhs, one being the head of the Hadith Department at al-Azhar University, and the other the Grand Mufti of the Republic.

The issue that the head of the Hadith Department was speaking on was, if you can believe it, the breast-feeding of adults, that is, a lactating woman producing her breast for suckling to a man, not a baby. As an example of this, he postulated a woman nursing her colleague at work behind closed doors. For his part, the Mufti, when asked about the permissibility of seeking blessing by touching the tomb of a righteous man such as the Prophet's grandson Hussein bin Ali, answered that it is permissible, citing as an example the companions of the Prophet drinking his urine for the blessing in it.

When we heard these two *fatwa*s we were stricken with disbelief; some laughed at their sheer strangeness, others refused to believe that such *fatwa*s were really uttered. When others were given a chance to comment on this, one of them (Sheikh Yusuf al-Qaradawi at a conference in Kuwait) said that such *fatwa*s can only be issued by sheikhs who are hired to serve the holders of power, and that such sheikhs only pronounce whatever those holding power wish to hear. This angered the Mufti, who was attending the same conference, and he replied that he was simply using *ijtihad* in expressing his opinion, meaning that he was only trying to express what he thought was right, and that whoever uses *ijtihad* and turns out to have given the right opinion is rewarded twice as much as he would be if he turned out to be wrong. This is to say that there is no harm in expressing one's opinion even if it may sound so strange.

The Grand Sheikh of al-Azhar did fire the man who issued the first of the two *fatwa*s, but we did not hear of any censure of the author of the second. Nor did we hear or read of any comment or clarification coming from the Sheikh of al-Azhar expressing his view on the two subjects of the *fatwa*s, on their having been issued at all, on the state of religious discourse they indicate, or on what he might do to avoid the issuing of such *fatwa*s in the future. Likewise there has not been any response from any other official, whether close to the religious establishment or to the prime minister, even though the issue seems to be grave enough to call for their intervention.

It seems to be grave for a number of reasons. We were all worked up about the Danish cartoons depicting the Prophet of Islam as a bomb-throwing terrorist, but, I think, these last two *fatwa*s do much more damage to the image of Islam and its Prophet than do the Danish cartoons. For, in the end, the cartoons came from a person who was not a Muslim and who obviously made a deliberate attempt at defaming Islam or may be connected with some influential people who had an interest in smearing Islam. Thus, to disclose such motives and connections may be sufficient to mitigate any adverse effects that might be caused by these cartoons. But what can one do when the head of the Hadith Department at al-Azhar University and the Grand Mufti of the Republic themselves mar the image of Islam, or when the Grand Sheikh of al-Azhar keeps quiet about one of the two awful *fatwa*s and does not make clear what displeased him about the other, or what he intends to do to prevent such *fatwa*s from being issued in the future?

To turn to the question of the social and psychological climate that could be responsible for the issuing of such *fatwa*s, one may note, for example, that Sheikh Hassan al-Banna, the head of Muslim Brotherhood in the 1930s and 1940s, never raised such concerns or expressed such views. Nor did we even hear the late Sheikh Mitwalli Sha'rawi (who was an immensely popular television personality in the 1970s) stirring up issues so far removed from people's real concern. Something must have happened during the last twenty years to change the general climate and public opinion in Egypt and allow such *fatwa*s to be issued.

4

At the annual Cairo International Book Fair, organized by the Egyptian General Book Organization, it has been noticed in the past few years that a large proportion of the books on display are religious publications that are very popular among the great majority of visitors. The fashion has extended even to the names of the bookshops participating at the fair: Piety, Light, Conviction, Virtue, Faith, and so on. So it was that when I came across a bookstore at the fair named The Religion Bookshop, I asked myself, "Is there really any other subject at the Book Fair?" Even the old bookshops that used to sell other kinds of books are now obliged to place publications that appear to have some relationship to religion at the front of their stalls, in the hope of attracting buyers to look inside. Loudspeakers broadcast Qur'anic verses at high volume or announce the release of this or that new volume of exegesis now available in electronic form.

One cannot have any doubt about the great majority of book fair visitors' true commitment to religion, their respect for everything associated with it, and their tight adherence to its observances. This is not only apparent in the great number of women wearing the *higab* or of men sporting beards, but also in the books which they page through, looking at their table of contents, and ultimately buying. From there, one must notice the transformations that have taken place in such manifestations of religiosity over the last few decades, which must also reflect the changes which occurred in the psychology and in the economic and social life of this segment of the population.

For one thing, one will note the changes that have occurred in the *higab* itself. True, many women, especially older ones, still prefer the veil that covers all of the hair, encircling the head like a tent and falling to mid-body to cover the hands. This one very much resembles the wimple of nuns. Often it is of the same color and cloth of the dress, which is itself long and loose, revealing no part of the body. This type of dress is still amply present, but what catches the eye is the sheer abundance of those wearing other types of the *higab*, especially girls and younger women. These *higab*s come in many colors and kinds of material, and are worn tightly round the head and face, framing it like a painting, so instead of distracting from the woman's looks they in fact call attention to them. They come below the chin and there stop abruptly, thereby covering nothing but the hair. If that is the case, what is to stop a little attention to the face with some make-up retouches here and there? Even more startling is the change in other articles of clothing, especially the pants now widespread among girls and women except those of advanced age. One should by no means make light of the popularity of wearing pants among the women of Egypt, for this does not go back more than about twenty years when an Egyptian woman wearing pants was a rarity, considered by many to transgress the bounds of propriety and due modesty. Women were then expected to wear long, loose dresses. Indeed, this was true even in the west until the 1960s, such that people would use the phrase 'wears the pants' to indicate the holder of authority in the family. This transformation of views on wearing pants, whether in Egypt or elsewhere, must be related to the greater emancipation of women, their growing participation in public life, and their occupation of jobs once restricted to men.

This increased participation of Egyptian women in public life could also be seen in the Book Fair in recent years, where women are seen taking part in various activities, from buying and selling to participating in symposia, to the manual labor of cleaning the streets of the fair, to handing out advertisements for all types of books and events. As the numbers of women participating in these activities grow, timidity is weakened, and women acquire greater courage and self-confidence.

A parallel change can also be noticed in the behavior of young men, which could be explained to some extent by the greater emancipation of Egyptian girls. Can young men's growing concern for their looks and grooming be explained by the increased public presence of girls? Egyptian boys' boldness in meeting girls and in complementing them, to say nothing of outright flirting, remains very limited, at least in the segment of society widely represented at the Book Fair, but it is not hard to find groups of boys in close proximity to groups of girls, sometimes only a few meters away, and to notice how their awareness of the girls' closeness exerts an effect on their behavior, not just in their keenness to present a good appearance, but also on their manner of speech.

Could this not also explain the appearance of a new type of preacher of the likes of, for example, Amr Khaled, a television preacher who has become exceedingly popular with the young? These preachers are 'modern' in more than one sense: in their style of dress and manner of speaking, and even in the topics they choose for their preaching. During my tour of the Book Fair grounds I came across a shop dedicated exclusively to the books and tapes of Khaled. On the cover of each book was a large photograph of its author, handsome and well dressed. I was tempted to buy some of the smaller and cheaper books of his, hoping to discover in the contents and the approach they take to religious subjects what might correspond to the picture of the author and explain his popularity among the young men and women of Egypt. So, what did I find? In the book entitled *Hubb Allah* (The Love of God), on page 15, the author says:

> I remember a young man of about eighteen years of age who went to one of the religious scholars of the ulama and said, "I am in a relationship with such-and-such a girl, we have done such-and-such things together; if I leave her, will that please God?"
>
> The man answered, "My son, if you do that, then He will not only be pleased with you, but you would improve your standing with Him."
>
> The young man swore to me, "When I went home I called her on the telephone and told her that I would not speak to her again because God is more precious to me than anything else." He then said, "I hung up the phone happy, and I felt something in my heart as if it were telling me, 'We shall exchange for thee a love with a much greater love.'"

Khaled's frequent use of words about love and desire is quite noticeable in this book in his discussions of "the love of Muslims for God." Such words must surely have had a different meaning for people in the early Islamic era than they do now after their frequent use in books, films, and songs, carrying different connotations to the new generation, far from the connotations usually meant by religious preachers.

It is clear that the young men and women of this generation have done everything they can to reconcile their families' traditions with the demands of contemporary life, and have managed various degrees of success in achieving this reconciliation. Thus, girls combine putting on the *higab* (after applying make-up) with wearing otherwise modern clothing. Where it comes to religious sentiments, both young men and women have tried as best they can, with the help of preachers of Khaled's type, to combine observance of their religion with the enjoyment of life, as far as their material circumstances may permit them. While they try to achieve greater material advancement than their parents or grandparents, and of which the contemporary media urgently tout the necessity and advantages, they also hope to preserve as much as they can of the traditions that their parents and grandparents have implanted in them.

In my stroll about the grounds of the Book Fair, I also made a great discovery: a bookshop of which I had neither heard nor seen before, named Jarir Books, after the name of an old classical Arab poet. A look inside revealed that everything on offer was a publication of a publisher with the same name. The first thing I noticed was the high quality of printing, the elegant covers, and expensive paper. More important were the subjects of the books, almost all of which revolved around success in life, in the worldly meaning of the quest for success. Among the books displayed, for example, was the venerable title that I first heard of at the end of the 1940s, when American culture first began to invade our lives: *How to Win Friends and Influence People* by the American author Dale Carnegie. We were told at the time that the book had achieved great success worldwide and sold millions of copies in different languages. Other books of this sort filled the shelves at Jarir Books, all of them presenting the same philosophy of life and all of them being translations of American authors, even though the first page of each opened with the *basmallah* (the opening invocation to every chapter of the Qur'an, but one).

Right next to Jarir Books was another stall selling nothing but computer discs with various types of instructional materials for ambitious young people to acquire new technical skills that could help them increase their income. One thing that caught my eye was a box-set of enticing colors depicting a girl wearing the *higab* with books at her side titled *Nuran Learns Languages*. Clearly the publisher hoped to attract a particular type of young person belonging to that segment of society inclined to name their girls Nuran (a name with a strong religious connotation).

One can clearly see that this attempt at striking a compromise between the traditional and the contemporary, the old and the new, is everywhere at the Book Fair. Even at the bookshops selling religious tomes one sees, along with the books explaining the performance of religious observances, bookshelves full of study guides intended to help students pass exams in various modern subjects. You can see this very clearly in the huge pavilion dedicated to computer programming: as soon as you walk in you are handed flyers about how to acquire computer skills by installment payments, or advertising the "most powerful computer dictionary," paid for in eleven monthly installments. But there are also flyers advertising religious recordings of every variety. All of this is taking place to the accompaniment of loud music blasting out of a computer placed right at the entrance to the pavilion, which is also broadcasting pictures on its screen of one scantily clad singer after another. Not far from this computer I saw a young veiled woman handing out flyers explaining the installment plan, almost dying from embarrassment at being required to stand in that location amid the throng of young men gathered to gawk at the screen.

10

Alienation

1

Every one of us has probably experienced a feeling of alienation at some period in one's life, of short or long duration. This could happen, for example, upon finding oneself in a new country where everything seems unfamiliar, or among people whose language one does not know, or who do not know one's own language. It is a painful feeling, sometimes too painful to bear. What about the disenchantment one might feel while remaining in one's own country, and in the midst of one's own family and friends? What could be the origin of the feeling of being alienated without leaving home? It must be that the home itself has changed the feeling that your country is no longer the same country, or that the people's pattern of behavior has changed so much that one, indeed, feels a stranger among them.

It is really not very hard to delineate many important changes that have come about in Egypt's political, social, and cultural life that might be responsible. I have already referred to some of them; but one is struck by the thought that the sentiment may not be the product of only a few years, but could go back to the beginning of the era of Mubarak, and even much further. To do full justice to the issue one may indeed have to go back to the beginning of the revolution of 1952. The reasons for disillusionment must, of course, have changed, and its intensity and the nature of the social groups that suffered most from it must have also varied from one period to another during the past sixty years.

Egypt's social and political life before the revolution had continued without radical change, and the faces of those running the political life in Egypt had remained virtually the same throughout the thirty years preceding it. If the king changed, his son took his place, and if the head of the most popular political party died, his closest follower would replace him. The economy continued to be run by the foreign occupying power; if it withdrew its forces from Cairo to reduce frictions, it settled nearby, along the Suez Canal. So, too, did the large landowners continue to occupy the top positions while, at the bottom, tenant farmers and agricultural wage earners continued to live not far from subsistence level. Between the two was a small middle class whose customs and values at the time of the 1952 revolution were not much different from what they had been at the beginning of the century. It is true that the overwhelming majority of the Egyptian people welcomed the revolution, and that a significant portion must have felt that the country had been returned to them, but one should also acknowledge that the revolution must have caused a strong sense of alienation in some sections of the population. This may not appear very important now and may not have appeared important then to many Egyptians, but the fact was that the royal family, the King's retinue, those with strong ties to the palace, and high-ranking officers likely passed through great humiliation, fear, and degradation, whether they remained in the country or left it to live abroad. Some sense of alienation must have also hit another segment of the population, one more patriotic, perhaps, than the royal family and court retainers. By this I mean the older politicized group of Egyptians whose hearts had long been set on the leadership of men like Saad Zaghloul and Mustafa al-Nahhas, and whose enthusiasm had been ignited in their younger days by the revolution of 1919.

This segment of the Egyptian population, which, although small, included a not inconsiderable proportion of the literati at the beginning of the 1950s, were surely taken aback to see a group of young officers taking the reins of power from much older men of much longer experience and greater education. Some of these men were naturally more willing to reach a compromise with the British and more prepared than the revolutionary officers to serve the interests of the large landholders, but no one could doubt the patriotism of those of them who took part in the 1919 revolution and were much more knowledgeable of Egypt's history and social problems than the new army officers.

This was enough to arouse some concern among this segment of Egyptians about the intentions of these army officers and to curb their enthusiasm for the revolution. These doubts were increasingly confirmed day after day, and their enthusiasm waned as they saw how those officers treated the leaders of the earlier era, and indeed their attitude toward Egyptian history as a whole. The new officers came gradually to treat the July Revolution not as the beginning of a new era in Egyptian history but rather as the beginning of this history. It looked as if they were making a deliberate attempt to erase Egyptians' memory of what had come before the revolution. Pictures of pre-revolution leaders were banished, no mention of them was made in the press, let alone news and pictures of the royal family. Songs with any connection in people's minds to that era—which was constantly being referred to as the 'bygone era'—were never again broadcast; patriotic songs that the new regime did not consider to be sufficiently 'revolutionary' met with a similar fate.

The events of July 1952 were first referred to by the new officers as a 'movement,' or sometimes as the 'blessed movement,' until it crossed the officers' minds to call it a 'revolution' and establish that name in perpetuity. Most Egyptians accepted this on the basis that what had begun as a military coup in 1952 had indeed been transformed by the important and radical steps that were taken afterward and brought great changes to Egyptian society. But, still, some Egyptian intellectuals who had witnessed the events of the 1919 revolution must have noted the differences between a true revolution, which swept all social classes along with it, and a movement undertaken in a twenty-four-hour period by a limited number of army officers, who then took the reins of power no more than four days later.

It must have pained this group of intellectuals to hear the new songs praising that group of officers, some of them using the same expressions once used to describe the deposed monarch, and to see them gaining in strength while pushing into obscurity those officers who were more in favor of democracy. Their sense of alienation must have also increased as they saw the way the new officers treated Egyptian intellectuals in general. The officers alleged, and took pride in saying, that they were against 'philosophizing' and that work was more important than words. They used to hold the men of the bygone era to scorn because they were good at talking but did nothing, whereas they (the officers) were able to transform ideas and hopes into law overnight. Thus, with a simple law abolishing titles, for example, they thought they could do away with the division of Egyptian society into classes. From the beginning the new rulers consulted with some carefully selected university professors who soon became indispensable and then were appointed cabinet ministers in their own right. When some of them seemed to the army officers to be inclined to 'philosophize' too much, slow to act, and to ask too many questions, they were replaced by other professors who were more prepared to co-operate with the officers. These were of a particular type, not necessarily the most respected by their university colleagues, something which further strengthened the feeling of alienation among university professors less willing to flatter the new rulers and less anxious to secure a high post.

It was during the early years after the revolution that the new rulers made up a distinction between 'men of expertise' and 'men of trust.' It was alleged that the revolution needed the former much less than it needed the latter. If the expert, scholar, or intellectual was 'uncooperative,' then a person of less experience and less knowledge was preferable as long as he was 'willing to co-operate.' This was another example of the preference for rapid change, even if not fully justified. And it was an additional source of alienation for those intellectuals who did not see the need for haste in dealing with important aspects of social life, such as education, culture, or economic policy.

The feeling of disillusionment among many Egyptian intellectuals became more intense when they saw the new regime appoint a young officer, who happened also to be a writer, as the official in charge of the High Council for Literature, Arts, and Social Sciences. They suddenly found themselves under the direction of a man much younger than themselves, with less of a literary standing, but who had greater understanding of the goals of the new regime, and was also quicker at taking decisions.

These alienated literati were not necessarily less enthusiastic about the measures taken by the new regime to reform the economy, develop industry, or to end the British occupation. The problem was not that they considered the regime unpatriotic, but rather that the regime made it very clear that it had no need for them. I once heard a prominent leftist intellectual in Egypt of the 1960s say, "The problem with Nasser is that he would not allow us to die for him." But the outcome was worse than that for the rest of the leftist literati, many of whom Nasser imprisoned for more than five years (1959–64) at the very time when he was putting into effect his well-known socialist laws. They were, thus, not only psychologically alienated, but also physically so. Their physical alienation came to an end with their release from prison in 1964, but their psychological alienation persisted.

When, in the mid-1950s, the regime suddenly announced that it had discovered that Egypt's true identity was Arab rather than merely Egyptian, neither I nor any politically engaged young Egyptian of my age had any objection to that. Why not? We were Egyptians, of course, but we were also Arabs. This discovery of Egypt's Arab identity seemed to us, at the time, not only very convincing, but also expedient. It presented the possibility of enhancing Egypt's ability, as well as that of other Arab states, to achieve their political and economic goals. It was not difficult, then, for my generation to recognize Arab nationalism as a worthy substitute for Egyptian patriotism. In that spirit we welcomed with joy the announcement in early 1958 of the union between Egypt and Syria to form the United Arab Republic, Egypt becoming merely the southern province of the new state. Nor did we mind the addition of two stars to the flag with which the new regime had replaced the old green flag inherited from the monarchical era, and which we used to salute when we were small. We accepted with good will the union with Syria, the change of our country's name, as well as the change of flag, but I doubt very much that this was the sentiment of the older generation who may very well have felt betrayed. This older generation did not deny that Egypt was part of a bigger Arab nation, or the many advantages of Arab unity, but I maintain that this sudden change in the conception of Egypt's identity must have caused many Egyptian intellectuals to feel something akin to alienation.

With the military defeat of 1967, the sense of disenchantment spread to include everyone, educated and uneducated, the elderly and the young, men and women, the political and the apolitical. Egyptians suddenly awoke to an urgent question: Was everything that happened after 1952 a deception? Was the "building of a strong army" a lie? Had the two missiles named "the Vanquisher" and "the Conqueror" been just a joke? Had all of the talk about liberating Palestine been a delusion? Of what use the talk about Arab nationalism and Arab unity if this was Egypt's true weight, with or without the other Arabs?

When Nasser announced that he accepted full responsibility for the defeat and that he would step down we were, of course, stricken with grief, but many people (and I among them) doubted very much whether the crowds who took to the streets, demanding that he should stay, did this spontaneously and were not pushed into it by the government's agents.

It was inevitable that we would then begin to hear repeated with oppressive tedium ungainly new slogans such as "no voice should be allowed to rise above the din of battle" or that "whatever was taken by force can only be returned by force." These simply added to our sense of alienation, as did calling the military defeat a "setback." We were not deceived by some high-ranking air force officer being brought to trial, neither were we convinced that the commander of the armed forces, 'Abd al-Hakim 'Amir, who committed suicide in prison (amid rumors that he had been 'suicided'), was the only one responsible for what happened. True, Nasser's funeral was marked by an unprecedented degree of awe and respect, and huge numbers came out spontaneously to bid him farewell with a genuine sorrow previously bestowed on few figures in Egyptian history. But in bidding Nasser farewell, the Egyptian people were really also bidding farewell to a period full of great hopes that had gone unfulfilled, and were shedding tears for what had befallen a nation in which they now felt themselves to be strangers.

2

The Egyptian people did not have much sympathy for the new president, Anwar Sadat, for Sadat was never really taken seriously by Egyptians during the eighteen years that had passed since the revolution. In fact, they may have regarded him as the least important and most lightweight of all the eighteen officers who had staged the revolution. Nasser had always installed him in positions that required more public-speaking skill than they did political savvy or personal courage. There was, of course, the puzzle that remains to be solved: Nasser's choosing him as vice president just a few months before his death. The mere fact that the Egyptian people regarded this as a mystery is enough to elucidate the public's true opinion of Sadat at the time.

It could not be expected, therefore, that the sense of alienation would disappear or even weaken, at least not during the first years of Sadat's rule. The people expressed this feeling in a number of ways, once in demonstrations that took place in 1972, demanding a war to retrieve the Sinai, and once by prominent authors and journalists signing a document that they presented to Sadat in the same year, also demanding war. During that time, the poet Ahmad Fuad Nigm and the blind lutenist Sheikh Imam were going around from house to house at the invitation of their many fans to sing some of their passionate poems, set to simple but affective music, all about the distress Egyptians felt at their ignoble defeat, lampooning the leaders who claimed to be protecting the nation while actually robbing it, and mocking those who claimed that the battle was ongoing with the appellation "Mrs. Battle Babble."

The Egyptian attack on Israeli forces on the east bank of the Suez Canal on 6 October 1973 was supposed to end the alienation between the people and the regime. But my observations of the feelings of the people, and my own personal feelings, tell me that that unspoken détente between the people and the regime did not last longer than a few days, even though Sadat continued to speak of the "Great Victory" until he was killed on 6 October 1981. Sadat described himself as the "Hero of War and of Peace," and many public institutions were given such names as "The Crossing" or "Sixth of October," and so on. Fundamentally, the explanation for the rapid failure of the Sadat regime to put an end to Egyptians' feeling of alienation was the obvious inconsistency between the military performance of 1973 and the political concessions that started to be granted immediately afterward, and persisted throughout the remaining years of Sadat's rule. It was possible to rejoice at Sinai having been returned (or about to be returned) to the Egyptians, even if only with partial sovereignty. But was this all that was needed to solve our problems with Israel: that Israel would take from us what it did not have before, then return part of it, whereupon we would be willing to forget that Israel took half of Palestine in 1948 and the other half in 1967? Sadat and his spokesmen talked unceasingly about the "expected peace" and the necessity of overcoming the "psychological barrier" that kept us from reconciliation with Israel, describing the October War as the "Final War," while repeatedly referring to the United States as the "American friend," and to Henry Kissinger as his "dear friend." This, in addition to him receiving in Egypt the Israeli Prime Minister and former terrorist Menachem Begin, as if he were also an old friend, widened the gulf between Sadat and the people. Then, again, Egyptians were startled one day by Sadat suddenly paying an official visit to Jerusalem in 1977 and at the sight of him laying a wreath at the tomb of the unknown Israeli soldier, followed by his signing of a peace accord in Washington in 1979 despite the warnings of some of his advisers and the resignation of one cabinet minister after another who refused to be part of such a move.

To the great majority of Egyptians, Sadat seemed determined to steer the course charted by the Americans no matter how contrary this was to Egyptian sentiments. When Sadat became so fearful that the opposition was getting out of hand that he imprisoned thousands of politicians, journalists, writers, and political activists in September 1981, up stepped an assassin who killed him as he stood at a military review one month later.

But the new kind of relationship that Sadat established with Israel was not the only reason for Egyptians' feeling of alienation under his rule. There were other sources of disillusionment, too.

Sadat opened many doors that had been closed in the days of Nasser, allowing a wave of westernization to sweep over Egypt's social life from every side, often with a crudity not at all agreeable to the tastes of a wide variety of Egyptians: leftist, nationalist, religious, or people with low and fixed incomes. All of these underwent a feeling of alienation unlike that which they had felt in the Nasser era. The surprising thing was that while many, or most, leftist intellectuals seemed willing to forgive Nasser for arresting them, for causing them to lose their jobs, and for depriving them of their right to express their political beliefs, they could not forgive Sadat for his way of opening the country to foreign goods, his partiality to foreign capital, his reversal of income redistribution, and for his new policies toward the United States and Israel. The religious and the nationalists were offended by his obvious carelessness with regard to preserving traditional values (despite his making a show of respecting them). Those of low and fixed incomes who had not been able to profit from the runaway inflation during the 1970s or to travel to one of the oil-producing states were nostalgic for the Nasser era, in which they had enjoyed more stability, or even an improvement, in their standard of living, and had much greater hope for the future.

Sadat's personality was very suited to this sudden wave of westernization. Since his early youth, he had been enamored of western consumer goods, American films, and every modern western technological device. This is seen in the many utterances to that effect in his autobiography while expressing his youthful ambitions and his hobbies, as well as in his dress, in his interactions with foreigners, and in the testimony of many who witnessed his great fascination with the western lifestyle every time he traveled to Europe or the United States many years before taking over the presidency. Although such personal characteristics may not have been a decisive factor, they likely played some role in the social and political life of Egypt acquiring some new features that were unfamiliar and distasteful to many Egyptians.

Take, for instance, the phenomenon of 'the First Lady of Egypt,' copied directly from the United States and unknown to Egypt, either in the earlier decades of the revolution or even in the monarchical era. King Farouk, like his father before him, was careful not to allow photographs or news of female royals to appear except on rare occasions. If Egyptians happened to see such pictures and saw the clothes the royal family wore, and the jewels with which the ladies adorned themselves, all giving an indication of the westernized lifestyle they led, they would not have found it so shocking, being, after all, the way kings lived. But things were different when they saw pictures of the wife of President Sadat repeatedly appearing in pictures showing her receiving high-ranking western politicians, heading conferences, or issuing statements and directives. Egyptians knew of her humble social background (as well as her husband's) and her limited education, and all this seemed to them not just unfamiliar, but also contrary to the ingrained habits of the Egyptian family. In contrast, Nasser's wife was, to the minds of Egyptians, much closer to their expected image of an Egyptian politician's wife, especially after a revolution that was staged in the name of the Egyptian people at large and not of a single privileged class. It seemed even odder coming from a regime calling for the adoption of 'values of the village.' When Mrs. Sadat's defense of her master's degree was broadcast on television, with three eminent professors as examiners and the president of the Republic in attendance, it looked very much like a staged event, with everyone agreeing beforehand what role to play, and all with the purpose of bestowing an additional honor on the wife of the president, who was not in need of any more honors.

The spread of the *higab* and modest styles of dress during Sadat's era created another source of alienation that one should not ignore just because those feeling it found that alienation hard to express. I am referring to the women of two segments of society: the first of these are women who grew up in a less conservative, more urbane environment and belonged to families which accustomed their women to a greater degree of freedom. It had probably never occurred to them or to their families that covering the hair and a particular amount of arm or leg was an indispensable condition for considering a woman of sufficient modesty. Such women, and they are many, have surely been overtaken by a sense of confusion and irritation on finding themselves in the midst of other women looking at them askance.

The other group is the Copts. It is not hard to imagine the degree of marginalization they must feel in this new climate, in which has suddenly spread this type of religious discourse that reaches them by loudspeaker and television screens, confirming the proliferation of the *higab* which a Coptic woman cannot wear, no matter how modestly she dresses, without feeling that she is denying her religion and her family's traditions.

A large segment of Egyptian intellectuals, too, resent this new type of fanatical discourse in which they see a glaring departure from the more tolerant interpretation of religion that prevailed in previous decades, and to which they had been accustomed. When they saw this new interpretation creeping into the media and into peoples' daily behavior and relations with each other, they, too, must have suffered a sense of alienation.

In the midst of all of these sources of alienation, some Egyptian intellectuals have preferred physical alienation to living in their own country. Some leftist intellectuals went to Baghdad or to Gulf states, or to Paris or London. They were welcomed by the Saddam regime, by leftist intellectuals in Paris, or by owners of Arabic language newspapers operating in London. A prominent Egyptian journalist preferred heading a Kuwaiti monthly magazine to being editor-in-chief of the largest daily newspaper in Egypt. Others sought easy jobs in another Arab country, where they had only to spend small amounts of their energy, even though they were deprived of the chance to express themselves. This at least guaranteed them peace of mind and rid them of the constant tension they felt in Egypt. Some Egyptian composers preferred to engage in commerce, while others chose to spend the rest of their lives raising cattle in their home villages.

When President Sadat was eliminated from the political stage on 6 October 1981, this was enough to make some Egyptians feel optimistic; that this involuntary removal of a president might incite the men of the new era to adopt policies different from those that the former president had taken, and which had led to such alienation between himself and his people.

Confirmation of this reversal did happen in the months immediately following the assassination. For only a few weeks had passed before Hosni Mubarak released the political prisoners that Sadat had recently imprisoned and allowed the opposition papers closed down by Sadat to begin publishing again. What is more, he prohibited the publishing of pictures of the president's wife except with special permission and within a few months the phenomenon of 'the First Lady of Egypt' had disappeared.

The president also expressed his determination not to visit Israel, and he gave the impression that he was going to be much more cautious in his relations with the United States than his predecessor, all creating a feeling among Egyptian intellectuals, and indeed among various segments of the population, that the alienation they were feeling might soon come to an end.

All this optimism began to wane, however, within a year of the new president's assuming power, and vanished completely by the early 1990s. It was already becoming clear when Israel attacked Lebanon in 1982 and Egypt remained silent, that the new president's stand toward Israel would not be any different from that of Sadat. The same conclusion could be made with regard to Egyptian relations with the United States, when President Mubarak looked completely helpless vis-à-vis American demands on Egypt concerning the American attack on Iraq in 1990.

Thus, by 1990 it became quite clear that the era of Hosni Mubarak was not going to be better than the Sadat era in any important issue of Egypt's foreign, Arab, or domestic policy. Then came the realization that things would not become any better regarding political freedom. It did not take long for the government to return to imposing restrictions on the press, by suppressing some papers and making deals with others, continuing to appoint the editors-in-chief for government newspapers, and appointing media officials more willing to implement the directives of power. To this was added continued interference in the elections to the People's Assembly and in the results of successive referenda. The phenomenon of 'the First Lady of Egypt' was also soon to return and it became clear that the First Lady of the Mubarak era was no less keen to play a role in public life than was the First Lady of the Sadat era.

Looking back over what has happened during the two eras, it all now seems quite comprehensible. What was required of Sadat was to change the direction of the ship, but once he did that there was nothing left for the new president to do save for some semi-routine work. And it seemed that this was very much suited to the personality of the incumbent president as compared to those of Sadat and Nasser. Nasser had introduced completely new foreign and economic policies, and he was, by temperament, bold enough to play that role. Sadat was directing Egypt in an entirely different direction, a job that was very much in line with his adventurous and mercurial personality. In contrast to these two presidents, Mubarak was by nature inclined to stability and to prefer the familiar to the new. In other words, with the coming of the era of Mubarak, the sacrificial lamb had already been slaughtered and all that remained was to flay and butcher it. So it happened in the Mubarak era that the concessions that Sadat had already agreed to with Israel and the United States were implemented one after the other, just as the assets of the Egyptian state were sold off piece by piece.

What happened was not only well-suited to the personality of the president, it was also suited to the personalities of most of the cabinet ministers and prime ministers who were to take office through the Mubarak era compared to their counterparts in the two preceding eras. The majority of those assuming the post of prime minister under Mubarak, and of those chosen as ministers, bore more of the characteristics of government employees than they did of politicians. Fouad Mohieddin, who was the last prime minister under Sadat and the first under Mubarak, was in fact the last prime minister of Egypt to possess some of the characteristics of a politician and who could boast of any political background at all. Indeed, successive prime ministers from the time Ali Lutfi assumed the post in the mid-1980s, and including Ahmad Nazif who held it twenty years later, were probably overcome by surprise when the post was offered to them, inasmuch as there was not a trace of political activity of any kind in their careers. As time passed, people lost interest in whoever took the post of a cabinet minister. Most of them had become mere employees, and not always very efficient ones at that, who had neither real interest in politics nor personal charisma that might have won for them some admiration. It is not surprising that these same characteristics also became prevalent among the editors-in-chief of the newspapers and magazines owned by the state. These were also chosen from colorless personalities with no known background in journalism to recommend them to such high positions. Some of them made use of ghost writers to pen their regular columns. One such editor-in-chief of the largest daily newspaper was made fun of by someone saying that "his writers outnumber his readers."

This was just what one would expect from a regime with no political vision and, even if it did have such a vision, no power to implement it; a regime devoid of both talent and vitality, that confines its role to implementing directives coming from outside. All of this was bound to strengthen the feeling of alienation among Egyptians in general, but the alienation under Mubarak has been somewhat different from that of the two previous eras. The discontent in the Nasser era was closely associated with fear; in the Sadat era, with anger; and in the Mubarak era, with depression. Egyptians are known to express their displeasure with their rulers by making sarcastic jokes, and the differences in the type of jokes of the three eras reflect this change. The jokes made about Nasser revolved around his police state and its secret intelligent services; those about Sadat made fun of his relations with Israel and the United States, as well as of his love for luxury. The jokes about Mubarak have revolved around a lack of talent and ability.

In this gloomy climate of great alienation, the government came out with a startling new notion that Egyptians had not come across before, neither after the July Revolution nor before it, and the very thought of it added to their feeling of alienation. This is the idea of bequeathal of the office of the president from father to son. The idea had never occurred either to Sadat or to Nasser, nor does it even resemble the inheritance of the kingship by the crown prince in a monarchical regime.

11

Mubarak's Successor

1

The political scene in Egypt in late 2010 seemed to be full of riddles and contradictions. Every day people saw proof that Egypt was a very soft state and at the same time a tough one. Soft to the point that it could not implement a judge's ruling or even enforce respect for traffic lights, but tough enough to be able to apply torture to people who dared oppose it and to shield those committing the torture from punishment. It was capable of bringing traffic to a halt and delaying people going about their private concerns for hours day after day, simply to clear traffic and provide security for some VIP who might be on his way to the airport to meet someone (not that important) or even to catch a plane to Sharm al-Sheikh for relaxation.

There is no shortage of evidence for how dictatorial Egypt's system of government had become. Laws were passed without being subject to serious discussions in parliament, like those extending the state of emergency (which has been in place since the assassination of President Sadat in 1981), while new prime ministers were suddenly appointed whom no one had expected and no one had elected. Very important international agreements were signed, such as the QIZ agreement with the United States and Israel, without hardly any open discussion, while billions of Egyptian pounds were spent on projects, such as the Toshka project, which should supposedly have added hundreds of thousands of feddans of new agricultural land, but to which all references stopped with no apology made for some serious errors of judgment. At the same time, certain opposition newspapers were surprisingly permitted to publish sharp criticism of the president, even personal criticism, without being closed down.

Someone reading the Egyptian papers would be confused as to whether the president was very strong or very weak. Every act was attributed to him, and every prime minister, speaker, or member of parliament had to begin his speech in praise of him. Every decision that was expected to please the people was attributed to the president. One wonders, therefore, of what use the ministers or the prime ministers were if they did no more than implement whatever came to the president's mind. But, apart from such declarations, there was no clear indication of the role he played in drawing up policies or in major acts of decision making. He seemed to be completely absent when a serious crisis faced the country, one requiring a major decision, such as an American or British attack on an Arab state, an Israeli attack on Lebanon, the sinking of a ferry full of Egyptian citizens, or a train catching fire and leading to the loss of hundreds of lives as a result of sheer neglect. In such situations, his pronouncements seemed to be extremely weak and no decisions were taken to reassure the people that such a thing would not be allowed to happen again or that the guilty party would be punished. Instead, he seemed to find the time and sangfroid during the crisis, or immediately after it, to attend some uncalled-for celebration or to watch a football match.

All the while, his son's star had been rising little by little as if the goal were to prepare the ground for him to take his father's place. The stops he made on his rise had been to hold certain fictitious positions created specially for him, with obscure titles that could be understood to include very important responsibilities, such as 'Head of the Policy Committee.' His statements were accorded exaggerated importance, even if he was merely repeating something that had already been said many times over. The statement would be placed on the front page of the papers with his photograph, a photograph chosen with great care to give the impression of great seriousness and decisiveness. It was as if there were a state administration especially established for choosing his photographs and crafting news connected to his name.

All of this happened while the father behaved as though he did not see what was going on, and if asked about it stoutly denied any intention of 'bequeathing office.' This also seemed to be a carefully crafted answer. Bequeathal usually involves the passing on of material holdings, which did not apply here, or of status under a monarchical system, which we also do not have. This was probably what the father meant by repudiating his intention of bequeathal. But what he failed to deny was precisely what we wished he would deny: that preparations were going on to insure that the result of any future referendum or election would be the replacement of father by son. That is precisely what the father was not prepared to deny.

2

The reader should not think that the idea of bequeathing the office of president grew in the mind of the president or his wife, or even in the mind of their son. There are numerous reasons for rejecting this notion, which we need not go into here. Indeed, even if the idea had originated in the presidential mansion, it would have been very easy for the president's advisers to turn the president and his family against the idea and to uproot it from their minds. The idea must have come to one of the members of this clique of advisers, who were the real holders of the reins of power, and pleased him greatly, whereupon he proposed it to the same group of advisers, who greeted it with enthusiasm and set about implementing it step by step. It seems to me that the thought process of this clique concerning bequeathal might have proceeded as follows: "President Mubarak is about to turn eighty, and he is starting to show signs of fatigue and failing health. This is hard to hide from the people, as when he was about to faint while giving a speech before the People's Assembly, forcing him to stop speaking and quickly leave the stage. Now, suppose he died suddenly, who would take his place? Any constitutional means for replacing the president is fraught with peril and is bound to place us—the real decision makers—in a dangerous predicament. There is no one we might consider, whom we would all agree on, to take up the office. Put another way, leaving the choice of a new president to the people who elect him from a field of candidates not set by us, might (indeed most likely would) lead to a new president who is hostile to us, or at least to a non-compliant leader who will not submit to our will. This could lead to an unhappy end to our influence, our wealth, and maybe even to our lives. We must find someone we can all agree on, someone we can be confident will continue implementing what we want done. It does not take much thought to realize that one of the president's sons is the one we need. The elder son is not appropriate because of his psychological make-up, so there remains none but the younger son.

"This younger son has many advantages: a young man, well-bred, does not remember his father except as president, or his mother except as First Lady. There is no malice in him and he knows nothing of our true goals. He may, of course, feel more comfortable with one or two of us than with the others, but there is nothing very harmful in this, and this is in any case what we could compete over. He has little or no experience of the guiles of people like us, and for that reason alone he can easily be persuaded that he possesses more good qualities than other Egyptians, that the great majority of Egyptians love his family and have great affection for his father and mother, and that the new order in the region (and even in the United States) is that the father leaves the presidency to his son (look at Syria and Libya)."

So, too, could they mention some genuine truths to help persuade him, such as that never in its history had Egypt's people really elected a president. "So why stop the course of history? Are you any less than your father, who came to the presidency without anyone having voted for him?" The means of persuasion are many, and if the job was to convince the son to accept becoming a president, nothing could be easier. There were some dangers, however, which could sabotage the plan. These dangers came from three sources: the United States, the Egyptian people, and certain members of the clique that surrounded the president.

This clique included some persons of whom the president's son was not very fond, or who may have done things to anger him. There were also those who knew all the scandals of the other members, something that could threaten the whole plan with failure. Such potential troublemakers had to be kept from staging a minor coup. Most people may have known nothing of this, but they would certainly have welcomed any fight among the members of the clique even if they did not know a thing about the reason for it.

But would the people accept the son as the new president? This was the second source of danger. No doubt this new plot was of an entirely new type in Egypt, regardless of the fact that the Egyptian people had never really elected their president before. Egyptians accepted with good will the hereditary throne that Muhammad Ali established in Egypt in the middle of the nineteenth century, at a time when most of the world was living under autocratic monarchies. Even so, Egyptians struggled to transform the system into a constitutional monarchy until they got the constitution of 1923 whereby the king 'reigned but did not govern.' Egyptians later accepted the autocracy of Nasser, acquiescing in his foreign and domestic accomplishments. If they found it hard to accept the transfer of rule to Sadat, who had been appointed vice president by Nasser, at least Sadat had some legitimacy for assuming the presidency by reason of his participation in the July Revolution. But he lost any legitimacy he once had when he started betraying one after another of the principles of the revolution and began faking elections.

The same applied to the rule of Hosni Mubarak, whom Sadat chose as his vice president without consulting anyone. Rigged elections continued, as did the attack on the principles of the revolution, until the revolution itself became a faint memory of a distant past. But for some, the attempt to transform the regime to one where power is bequeathed from father to son, which was entirely new to Egypt, was also something that the Egyptians found utterly hateful.

Knowing all of this and understanding the full extent to which Egyptians must have detested this plan, where did the clique that held the rudder of government in Egypt find the nerve to try to impose it on Egyptians? This was an idea that could never have occurred to a man like Sadat, with all his lack of regard for legitimacy and constitutionality. Nor could it have occurred to Nasser, despite his great popularity. The answer, in my opinion, comes down to differences in the personalities of the three presidents, to the nature of their relations with those immediately around them, and to the changes that occurred in Egypt in the interim.

Nasser was undoubtedly a political man in every sense of the word; politics occupied his thoughts and filled his life. Sadat was a different kind of man, much less serious, quite keen on the small pleasures of life and having no scruples about the various benefits that his post brought to him and to his family. Sadat was also a political man, but his understanding of politics was rather primitive, indeed close to that of a village headman, and he was often in a hurry to solve political problems to be free to please himself. As far as could be seen, Mubarak was less keen on the enjoyment of the good life, but he also had even less patience than Sadat with political problems. For that reason, he seemed to welcome any chance to pass the burden of political decision-making to someone else.

Such personality differences were reflected in how each of the three viewed his office. While Nasser took the post with the utmost seriousness,

Sadat took it with a mixture of seriousness and levity. For Mubarak, being president was merely a matter of fate, and he did not seem to know exactly how it had come to him.

There was also a difference in the relationship each of the three had with the men close to them. Nasser was without a doubt the ultimate authority. He would listen to the opinion of some of those close to him, but only when he asked for it. In any case, he was always able to distinguish between constructive opinions and useless or harmful ones, and it was very difficult to deceive him by depicting something that was really meant for one's private benefit as being for the good of the country or the president himself. It was easier to deceive Sadat, if only because of his love of the good life and his distaste for the burdens of office. But Sadat was better than his successor at understanding the motives of those around him and at guessing the real reasons behind their advice.

Despite criticisms that might be made of frequent violations of the law under Nasser, this was indeed insignificant compared to the lawbreaking that occurred under the two succeeding presidents. This must surely be related to the personalities of these presidents and of the men close to them, but it must also be strongly connected to the economic Open Door policy (infitah) implemented by both. The infitah was inevitably associated with greater pressure from foreign economic interests and with a higher rate of inflation, both of which favored less law-abiding behavior.

All of this would surely have weakened the principle that had prevailed in Egypt since Muhammad Ali founded the modern Egyptian state two centuries ago, namely that of separating the public domain from the private, and public funds from those of the ruler. Gradually, more and more state holdings were treated as if they were private property, and actions that had once been regarded as egregious crimes were repeatedly ignored. It looked as if Egypt had returned to the depredations of the Ottoman and Mamluk eras.

In just such a climate, the idea of the bequeathal of the office of president appeared—not very different from the premise of expropriating public land, granting state prizes to people whose sole claim to them is their connection with high officials, or permitting the CEO of a publicly owned newspaper to use his office as a means of amassing a fortune, and so on. Nothing of this sort would have been permitted under Nasser, and hence it could never have occurred to Nasser to bequeath the presidency to one of his sons. Under Sadat, excessive violation of the law was still a new phenomenon so it was unlikely that Sadat would think of taking such a step, but, even if he did think of it, the consideration of the harm that such a decision was bound to bring him would have been sufficient to stay his hand. Meanwhile, by the end of two decades of the Mubarak era, the mixing of the public and private domains had reached the point where the idea of passing on the presidency was at least conceivable. To this was added, no doubt, the increased influence of the power elite surrounding the president, supported perhaps by a slight nod of approval from the president.

All of this aside, convincing Egyptians of the bequeathal would no doubt prove a very difficult job. To be sure, the law was flouted one hundred times a day and public funds were frequently intermingled with private wealth, but that the son of the president of the Republic might inherit the office of the presidency from his father, without his possessing any distinguishing feature that might better suit him to the position than millions of other Egyptians, such a proposition was very difficult to accept. At the same time, as I have explained, the matter was one of life or death for the clique around the president. That being the case, the strategy deserved expending every effort to see it accomplished, even while exercising all due caution and circumspection.

Apprising Egyptians of the matter was, however, not enough; the Americans, too, would have to agree. It is impossible to imagine that such a matter could go forward without their approval; they were in a position to ruin the whole plan if it did not please them. How to get them to say yes?

To some degree or another, the Americans must have been concerned about how the Egyptians would accept the hand-over. Such concern would not, indeed, have arisen from their excessive devotion to democracy or their respect for the wishes of the Egyptian people (that much should be obvious at least to the power elite in Egypt). Their main concern would have been that Egyptians' resentment over the inheritance could lead to unrest, rioting, or what American politicians usually refer to as 'instability.' Such 'instability' would be undesirable to the Americans in that it might obstruct the opening of Egyptian markets to American goods, services, and investment, or the realization of the American–Israeli plan for the Arab region.

By hook or by crook, then, the Egyptian power elite had to convince the Americans that there was nothing to fear. They had to convince them that Gamal Mubarak commanded the love and respect of the Egyptians, or at least that such love and respect would come gradually after he inherited office, or even that it would be an easy thing for Egyptians to love Gamal

Mubarak if the Americans gave him a helping hand. It could be done, for example, through a huge gift from the Americans to the Egyptians, to be given, perhaps, first to Gamal Mubarak for him to then present it to the Egyptian people. They could also try to convince the Americans that passing the presidency from father to son would further American goals and not hinder them. Or they could present the president's son as the person most inclined to, say, extend American-style education in Egypt, or to promote a love for the American lifestyle and other attitudes favorable to American business interests. Where else would they find a president with such qualifications?

The Egyptian power elite must have been trying to convey such a message to the U.S. administration for some time. What could possibly have been the American reaction?

3

We should never doubt that the American administration must have known pretty well what was going on in the minds of the clique that held the reins of power in Egypt. After all, these men were themselves a creation of the American administration, which had singled them out, tested them, and culled the unfit from among them. Reports must have been written daily or monthly to Washington on their behavior, the size of their fortunes, and what might be used against them should it become necessary.

Any other depiction of how the American administration views the ruling elite in Egypt does not square with the notion of a great power managing the affairs of a good part of the world and possessing the power to know the minute details of what might affect its vital interests. To be sure, the American administration must sometimes make mistakes, either as a result of false information or of some special interests within the United States itself trumping the greater interest of the country. But one must expect that a swift correction of mistakes and a return to sound decision-making would usually be made. By sound decision-making, I mean, of course, whatever realizes the greater interest of the United States at any particular moment in time.

I have already indicated that a government such as that of Ahmad Nazif seemed perfectly suited to serving American interests in Egypt during the Mubarak presidency. If we moved one step up to those close to the president, it was very likely that the U.S. administration did not have the inclination to change them, at least not until the crises of Iraq, Iran, Syria,

Lebanon, and Sudan came to end—crises for which the U.S. administration did not seem to have easy solutions. As long as easy solutions were not forthcoming, the American administration would probably have preferred that this clique remain in place, for, as the English saying goes, "don't change horses midstream."

But, until the time came for a change, what was the ideal stand toward the bequeathal of the president's office from the American point of view? From time to time, one got the impression that the U.S. looked favorably on Gamal Mubarak's taking various responsibilities and it sometimes dealt with him as if he were indeed the next president. But, at other times, one heard comments to the effect that the American administration was taking a 'neutral stance' on the issue, considering it a purely internal matter in which it did not like to interfere. At still other times, we saw or heard what could be understood to mean that the United States was determined that the president be chosen democratically. Meanwhile, the Egyptian power elite seemed to change its tactics from one moment to the next, perhaps as the American stance itself changed.

It is easy to see why giving contradicting signals to the Egyptian regime was probably the best attitude for the American administration to take to the issue of hand-over. The U.S. administration no doubt knew very well that there were hundreds or thousands of people besides Gamal Mubarak who could occupy the position of president in Egypt and continue to serve American interests. But Gamal Mubarak might also serve these interests, and he, too, was not lacking in the requisite positive qualities. The advent of Gamal Mubarak was not, however, without its difficulties. But what could the American administration gain by expressing a final opinion on this issue right away, before the end of the phase of the reordering of the Middle East? Actually, it seemed best to leave the administration's position ill-defined, by alternately using phrases such as "looking with sympathy on the matter," or, "we find no strong reason to object at this time," or, "the time is not right for taking a final decision in this regard," or, "stay the course until a suitable solution may be found at the appropriate time," and such like. In other words, American interests were probably best served by keeping the Egyptian power clique in a state of anxiety over what the final American position might be. This would help keep them in line and motivate them to do exactly what the Americans wanted them to do with regard to the ongoing crises of Iraq, Iran, Lebanon, Syria, Sudan, and, of course, Palestine.

Such a depiction of the American stance may seem too cruel, but when did the American administration ever refrain from taking such a position when it deemed it necessary to realize the higher interests of the United States?

But if the American administration seemed to understand the motivations of the Egyptian power elite toward the issue of bequeathal of office, this power elite seemed also to understand full well why the U.S. took the position it did on this issue. Each side seemed to understand the other well, playing a game of attack and defense, now warning and threatening, now back-pedaling and searching for reconciliation. And all of this was being played out over the heads of Egyptians, without their being party to this infernal game. This calls to mind the children's game 'monkey-in-the-middle,' in which two players try to keep a ball away from a third standing between them; as the two pass the ball back and forth between themselves, the third tries his best to intercept it. The game of bequeathal was played out between the Egyptian power elite, the party interested in the bequeathal, and the American administration, which had an entirely different set of goals and considerations. Meanwhile the Egyptian people stood pitifully by, having almost lost hope of ever catching the ball, of which they were, after all, the true owners.

If this analysis of the motivations and interests of the two sides in the political game in Egypt is correct, it is possible to understand much of what was going on in the final months of the Mubarak presidency, which may otherwise have appeared very puzzling. In the game of monkey-in-the-middle, the player holding the ball feigns his intention to throw the ball to the player in the middle, but instead throws it to his teammate, whereupon the two laugh demonically. Much of what passed as discourse between the Egyptian regime and the Egyptian people or between the American administration and the Egyptian people was nothing more than that game between the Egyptian regime and the American administration. Thus, the American administration might say, "Let there be democracy, even if it leads to the Muslim Brotherhood coming to power." Then the Egyptian regime would answer, "Of course, Sir, that is exactly what we shall do." Thereupon, the regime would allow a crack in the door to let a few members of the Muslim Brotherhood through, and then slam it in the face of the rest, beating them and throwing them in jail. Then the American administration would say, "Let there be freedom of the press," and the Egyptian regime would answer, "Of course! Just you watch how we allow the opposition papers to go as far as to attack the president and his family." Whereupon the editor-in-chief of an opposition newspaper would get beaten and thrown out of a car into the desert, while one journalist after another was hauled before the courts, and the American administration bestirred itself not, as though the issue were of no concern to it. Then the American administration would intone, "Let there be freely contested elections for the presidency." And the Egyptian regime would answer, "Of course, of course! Here are Ayman Nour[12] and Nu'man Guma'[13] to stand on equal footing with the president in the elections." But elections were not even held before one of them was caught in a scheme to discredit him, which resulted in his complete withdrawal from political life, and the other was put in jail, even though he had been the darling of the Americans only a few months earlier. Here again, Washington made a show of protest without exerting any effort to rescue their man. As for all the repetitive and useless talk about amending the constitution and amending it yet again, it was designed merely to play with Egyptian minds while at the same time making a show of a semblance of democracy to the Americans.

Throughout all of this, pictures of Gamal Mubarak would appear everywhere and then disappear. In photographs taken of footballers who had just achieved a big win abroad, Gamal Mubarak would be there to bask in the glory; then, when it seemed advisable, his pictures would disappear from the papers until the next appropriate occasion. Meanwhile, the regime would adopt an enormously weak stand toward the running crises in Iraq, Iran, Lebanon, Syria, and Sudan, completely in line with the will of the American administration.

This devilish game was suddenly brought to a very unexpected end by the uprising of 25 January 2011. It took a little more than a week for President Mubarak to appoint a vice president and to announce that he did not intend to stand for election at the end of the period of presidency ending in September 2011; less than another week passed before the vice president announced that Mubarak's son was not to stand for election either. The reasons behind this dramatic change are not difficult to guess. It must have been known to everyone concerned how unpopular this succession from father to son was to the Egyptian people. And the people's wishes had suddenly turned into a real threat to the regime's very survival.

12

Egypt and the Arabs

1

Many people, in Egypt and elsewhere, have for a long time noticed and commented on the gradual erosion of Egypt's place in the Arab world. Egyptian intellectuals are pained by the memory of the day when Egypt behaved and was treated rather like the mother hen of the rest of the Arabs. Egypt was the 'mecca' of Arab politicians before they took an important decision in their relations with another Arab state, or with one of the great powers, or even with regard to some important aspect of their own domestic affairs. What has happened exactly to change all this?

The Arab leadership no longer goes to Cairo except occasionally, or, if they do, it will be for a social call or to attend some ponderous meeting that everyone knows beforehand will be fruitless. If Egyptian politicians go to another Arab country, it is rarely for the purpose of reaching a solution to some problems of that country; indeed it is usually in the hope of solving some problem of Egypt itself (often a financial problem), or to deliver a message coming from some non-Arab party.

In the mid-twentieth century it was often said that "the Egyptians write, the Lebanese publish, and the Iraqis read." The saying still holds literally, of course, but the meaning has been greatly transformed. Even though Egyptians still do write, they no longer hold the place of leaders of Arab political thought, social studies, or historiography (and, I daresay,

159

also of Arabic literature). The names of such writers as Taha Hussein, 'Abbas al-'Aqqad, Tawfiq al-Hakim, and others were known to every Arab household up to the 1950s; then the names of Naguib Mahfouz, Yusuf Idris, and Ahmad Bahaa al-Din became well-known throughout the Arab world in the 1960s and 1970s. Nowadays, it is hard to find an Egyptian name having such status in the Arab world. A Yemeni intellectual was once speaking to me about the old Egyptian weekly *al-Thaqafa*, a literary magazine of the highest quality, telling me that a few copies of it used to arrive in Sana'a during the 1940s to be snatched up and passed from hand to hand by Yemeni intellectuals, whence it would be taken to other Yemeni cities. If a copy ever returned to its owner in Sana'a, it would come back dog-eared from the many hands that had held it. If I ask myself which Egyptian magazines could now occupy the place that *al-Thaqafa* once did in the 1930s and 1940s, whether inside or outside Egypt, I would not be able to name one. Is the venerable Egyptian monthly *al-Hilal*, which is today more than 120 years old, better now or is it the Kuwaiti *al-'Arabi*? I cannot say, neither can I say whether the Egyptian daily *al-Ahram*, also of august history, bears more weight today than the Saudi-owned *al-Hayat*, published in London.

What has happened with other media has also been quite embarrassing to Egyptians. The Egyptian radio station, Voice of the Arabs, deserved the name in the 1960s, but the world has changed a great deal since those days; television has taken the place of the radio, and satellite television has entered every Arab home. Tiny little Qatar has been able to draw audiences away from Egyptian television stations, and its news channel, Al Jazeera, has won much more credibility than that enjoyed by any Egyptian news broadcaster.

Many are the signs of decline, and many are also the explanations, some less painful to Egyptians than others. One is simply that it is the way of the world that some Arab states were bound to overtake others, sooner or later reaching the level that Egypt had attained in the field of cultural and social advancement, and even surpassing it. The gap between Egypt and other countries in terms of college graduates could not simply have remained as it had been at mid-twentieth century, and this had inevitably to be reflected in the cultural production and the media of each country. At the middle of the last century, when Kuwait wanted to publish a monthly cultural magazine (*al-Arabi*) it was indeed obliged to hire an eminent Egyptian journalist and scholar as its editor-in-chief. In the

1970s, it was again obliged to hire another prominent Egyptian writer as editor-in-chief of the same magazine to replace the first. By the beginning of the 1980s, Kuwait was able to free itself from Egypt in this regard and depend upon itself.

All of this may explain how other Arab countries caught up with Egypt, but it does not explain the decline of Egypt itself. To be sure, new universities have been built in every Arab country, but what does that have to do with the decline in education at Egyptian universities? Yes, the number of newspapers, magazines, and television stations has increased in the Arab world, and their professional standards have risen, but there has also been a decline in the media inside Egypt, which must be part of the reason for the Egypt's waning place in the Arab world.

There is, of course, the economic factor, and it is important. In the mid-twentieth century, Egypt had the highest per capita income in the Arab world with the exception of Lebanon. Now it has the lowest per capita income, with the exception of Somalia, Mauritania, and Yemen. A higher per capita income is usually reflected in the greater ability to develop the country's military power, to increase its political influence, and to advance its education and cultural life. Following the defeat of 1967, which had disastrous effects on the Egyptian economy, the Egyptian president was compelled to request economic aid from this Arab monarch or that, and this economic dependence must have contributed to the decline in Egypt's political influence.

While the Egyptian economy was getting weaker, the Egyptian state was also getting increasingly 'soft,' as I have tried to explain earlier in this book. A 'soft state' is necessarily a bad leader: it is less reliable during a military or political crisis, less capable of enforcing its will, and its intellectual production suffers in standard and creditability. This has become increasingly apparent in the development of Egyptian–Arab relations during the last forty years.

2

Startling evidence of the decline in Egypt's position vis-à-vis other Arab states came about in a horrible accident that occurred in September 2005. One can confidently assert that such an incident could not have happened or even been imagined twenty or thirty years before. Two young men decided to hold an auto rally; one was an Egyptian university medical student of around twenty years of age from a family of professionals in

Tanta, whose mother was a hospital director and his sister a doctor; the other a Qatari from the ruling family, the bearer of a diplomatic passport, not older than eighteen. The Egyptian drove a new BMW and the Qatari drove a brand new Ford. The rally took place on the road leading to Cairo Airport, one of the main roads in Heliopolis, and the accident occurred at 1:08 in the morning. There must have been several other cars still coming and going along the airport road, and many young people and families were still out on the strip of grass in the middle of the highway, enjoying a bit of breeze on one of those hot and humid Cairo nights.

The two young men apparently decided to race without consideration for traffic laws, or the fact that they were endangering the lives of other people coming from or going to the airport, or sitting on the green strip of grass in the middle of the road. Indeed, a relative of one of the victims said that he saw a police car sitting by the side of the road at the starting point of the race. No one knows exactly what the police car was doing there. Was it there to give the two racers protection from any protest that might be made against the race? It appears that the Egyptian beat his Qatari competitor, who, angry at this, sped up to faster than 200 kilometers per hour. People saw his car almost take flight only to come down on the green in the middle of the road, killing five people and injuring eleven others, who were rushed to hospital.

The two racers fled. It later became known that the Qatari left for his country the next day at 8:30 a.m. on an EgyptAir flight, that is, more than seven hours after the accident. What we do not know is what the Egyptian police were doing throughout that time, or what the airport authorities or the officials at EgyptAir were doing either. Why was the name of the Qatari youth not added to the no-fly list until 11:19 p.m. on Friday night, almost twenty-four hours after the accident? The Egyptian youth stayed hidden for two weeks, during which time, it was alleged, the Egyptian police had been unable to find him in spite of their knowing everything about him. Then he surrendered to the police and told the investigating officer the same tall story that he had told his mother to explain his presence at the scene of the accident. He claimed to have no connection with the accident at all, but was merely passing by and had stopped to see what was happening when, angered at the speed of the Qatari driver, he set off in pursuit, which is why his car had suffered a small scratch, which he then repaired. Perhaps that is why it took him a whole two weeks to reappear.

Leaving aside the two race drivers, consider what happened to the others. The ambulance came after fifty minutes, according to the father of one of the injured, without the necessary first-aid equipment. Thus the injured continued to bleed while the vehicle was taking them to the hospital. En route, the ambulance attendants would avail themselves of some of the valuable possessions of the injured (according to one of their relatives), such as their mobile telephones which were never to be seen afterward. One of the injured was refused entry into a government hospital on the grounds that his injuries were too bad to treat. And when another was taken to a private (so-called 'investment') hospital, his injuries were not to be examined until he paid one thousand Egyptian pounds against the bill. That kind of money was hard to find at that time of night and in the face of such an unexpected accident. For it is most unlikely that a young man going off to enjoy the breeze along 'Uruba Street on a hot night could foresee that the car of a Qatari youth would land on top of him in the middle of the road.

The daily papers could not ignore an accident of this type, however embarrassing to everyone. So they published the news on the first day with as brief a coverage as possible. Even then, people's emotions were stirred to the extent that the newspapers were obliged to follow the developments of the story day after day, but with many considerations and sidebars, hoping therewith to calm people's feelings. So it was said, for instance, that the Qatari youth had been arrested and was now in prison in Qatar. (Was that really the expected fate of a young man from the Qatari royal family?), and that communications were under way between the Egyptian and Qatari governments. (I wonder what type of communications they were, and in what spirit the Qatari government received the call from the Egyptian authorities on this matter in the light of the repeated requests from the Egyptian government for aid from Qatar?) This manner of official news reporting was sufficient to make the readers lose all trust in whatever was reported of further developments in the case, such as announcing that the Egyptian president or ministers were closely following the condition of the injured, or that the Qatari youth was placed in custody in his country, or that the Qatari authorities had welcomed the idea of receiving representatives of the Egyptian prosecutor's office in Qatar to participate in the investigation, and so on. Among the startling statements attributed to the investigating authorities in Egypt was that they had requested the extradition of the young Qatari man, adding that "if they refuse, then let them accept that an Egyptian delegation would arrive in Qatar to follow up the investigation."

Such being the state of affairs, when I heard that the very popular chat show 'Make Yourself at Home' (al-Beet beetak) would include a segment on this accident featuring the father of one of the killed and the father of one of the injured, I was keen on watching it. At the start of the program we were shown a famous actress being questioned about her private affairs. This was repeatedly interrupted by advertisements, such as one with a young Lebanese singer drinking Coca-Cola, another with a boy in a folk neighborhood touting Seven Up, and so on. Another advertisement offered a prize of an appliance worth ten thousand Egyptian pounds to the person who knew the capital of Bangladesh, another prize of a Mercedes Benz automobile, and a grand prize of the ownership title to an apartment . . . , and such like, all offered by a mobile telephone service and winnable by calling a certain mobile telephone number. All the while, viewers were advised that each mobile telephone call would cost one and a half Egyptian pounds.

I asked myself, in the midst of this wonderful festival of advertisements for such delightful goods, and conversations with such famous actresses, and all the promises of fine prizes, if there would really be a segment about the airport road accident and if a father of one of the victims would really accept to appear on such a show. But the segment did come, and the fathers of the victims did appear, their faces showing signs of grief and confusion. They talked with great boldness, wondering in what kind of state such an accident could happen while the perpetrator could flee with such ease.

Here was a very serious subject, and extremely upsetting, being discussed, repeatedly interrupted by advertisements about soft drinks and following chitchat about the private lives of some actresses, with viewers enticed to keep watching by the chance of acquiring an apartment, a car, or ten thousand pounds through sheer luck; good luck being presented as the only solution possible for their problems. Throughout it all was a new scam by which the mobile telephone companies would realize huge profits through the cost of the calls from millions of Egyptians who no longer had any hope of solving their problems except by such miserable means. The program even had the audacity to cut away from the father of one of the victims who had died in the accident to some advertisements, one of which showed the Lebanese singer touting Coca-Cola, and then come back to resume the talk about what had happened to the young man before he died. This, then, is how Egyptian television mixes up the serious with the frivolous, the tragic with the trivial, leaving viewers in a state like lifeless corpses, devoid of mind and conscience.

In any case, what the advertisements, prizes, and chats with actresses did not accomplish, the program managed to the next night by broadcasting statements from the minister of health, the attorney general, and even from the president of the Republic. They expressed their utmost concern about the subject, assured viewers that they were following developments in the case minute by minute, and were taking all necessary steps to protect the dignity of Egypt and Egyptians by securing the rights of the dead and injured. The announcer became quite emotional as he read out the president's words about the accident, saying that he regarded all the victims as his own children and expressing his determination that the investigation should take its course without relinquishing any of the rights of the Egyptians. He ended by announcing his decision to treat all of the injured at state expense. I said to myself, "So this is how the program 'Make Yourself at Home' is closing the story: a happy ending, even if a fabricated one, followed by praise of the president."

The next day I read in the daily papers the words of the foreign minister concerning the accident. He assured Egyptians that the Qatari youth would appear before the court in Qatar, and that the Egyptian Foreign Ministry had informed the Qatari embassy in Cairo of "Egypt's demand for such an action." But he also chided Egyptians for what seemed to him to be their "over-sensitivity" toward the whole incident. For my part, I thought that all that Egyptians needed in order to get over such "over-sensitivity" was to go through another ten years like the last twenty or thirty. The youth of Qatar, and perhaps all Gulf youth, may rest assured that they will be able to race again along the streets of Heliopolis and other neighborhoods of Cairo, having dispensed with any feelings of sympathy Egyptians might feel for one another. No doubt assisting them in that regard will be the Egyptian television's broadcasting of programs and advertisements that would work toward the elimination of any sensitivity that may remain.

13

Egypt and the United States

1

For nearly thirty-five years, Egypt has kept saying yes without deviation to whatever the United States asks of it: in its foreign policy, its policy toward the Arabs, its relations with Israel, and its economic policy. The result has been a continuous decline in Egypt's political and economic standing internationally and within the Arab world while Israel has been increasing its gains at Egypt's and Arab expense. If this is indeed the case, why did Egypt find it so difficult to say no to the United States?

It is not, as many may think, the huge economic burden that Egypt would have had to carry if American aid had been suspended. For the truth is that what is called 'American aid' to Egypt, as is probably the case with any so-called foreign aid given by a large country to a poor one, involves a large deception, as the following points show in the case of Egypt.

First: When American aid returned to Egypt in 1975, after having been suspended for nearly ten years, the Egyptian economy passed through two stages. The first was a stage of about ten years (1975–85) that was characterized by rapid economic growth, driven not by American aid but by the remittances of Egyptian migrants to the Gulf following the great increase in oil prices of 1973–74. This was accompanied in turn by reduced pressure on the labor market, which was then able to absorb a large number of surplus workers. The next twenty years (1985–2006) saw what was probably

Egypt's worst economic performance of the twentieth century, with the exception of the years of the world economic crisis in the 1930s and the eight years following the 1967 war, whether with regard to income growth or the deterioration in income distribution and employment. All of this happened in the midst of a flood of American foreign aid, in per capita terms exceeding all American aid to any other country except Israel.

Second: American military aid to Egypt has not been associated with any improvement in Egypt's political position, neither in the world as a whole nor in the Middle East; indeed, Egypt's status in the region has definitely declined. Egypt made no military move to assist Iraq when its nuclear reactor was hit by Israel in 1981, or to assist Lebanon when Israel attacked it in 1984 and again in 2006, or to assist Libya when American planes bombed it in 1986. In other words, American military aid did not strengthen Egypt either militarily or politically; if anything, it weakened Egypt in both fields.

Third: The direct causes of Egypt's economic weakness (and poor performance) during the last three decades may be summarized by a very low rate of saving, a persistent balance of trade deficit, and the weak performance of the two main commodity sectors: agriculture and manufacturing. These three failures go a long way toward explaining the low growth rate in the national output and the high rate of unemployment. But the low savings rate and the balance of trade deficit can in turn be attributed largely to the application of an inadequate model of Open Door policies, which persists until now. It is also easy to see the relationship between the application of this model and Egypt's submission to American will ever since it was applied. The weak performance of agriculture and industry can be partly explained by the state relaxing its role in those two sectors, an essential part of the model not only encouraged but virtually demanded by Washington. The laxity of domestic and foreign private-sector investment in those two sectors can also be attributed to the fact that under the new economic policies, much higher rates of profit were bound to prevail in the service sectors, such as tourism, commerce, and entertainment, than in the manufacturing and agricultural sectors. The largest part of foreign private investment in the past thirty years has been directed at these high-profit sectors or the petroleum sector, which have weak impact on the level of employment. Meanwhile, the foreign investment that took the form of privatization contributed little to growth and caused increased unemployment.

The poor performance of the Egyptian economy has therefore been closely associated with the strengthening of ties between Egypt and the United States. What is it, then, that prevents Egypt from refusing American aid and reducing its economic ties with the United States?

The answer is: pure force. In other words, we do not say no to the United States not because of the great harm we would suffer if America abandoned us, but simply because we are forced to say yes. Such force takes the familiar form seen in the large majority of examples of colonial relationships, both old and new, where coercion is not exercised directly by the hand of the colonizer but at the hand of his local agents. This kind of indirect coercion is obviously not new. Colonizers have always made use of it because it is less expensive in blood and money. In addition, the local agents are able to address the coerced in their own language and are better able to dupe them through the various means of media deception, and they may even succeed in depicting this rule by proxy as genuine Egyptian rule.

There are some similarities between Egypt's relationship with the U.S. at the beginning of the twenty-first century and its relationship with Great Britain in the seven years between the end of the Second World War and the staging of the revolution in July 1952. The king could not call upon a politician to form a government if the British did not approve it. Nor could the government follow an economic or foreign policy that was not to the liking of the British. Britain did not rule Egypt directly but through the king's retinue and minority parties. In the same way, the Americans now rule Egypt through the president's advisers and a very small clique sitting atop the National Democratic Party. The British had a token force in place to remind the rulers of Egypt that they could not disobey the powers that be and so do the Americans today. For the British, this token power was stationed in downtown Cairo at the Qasr al-Nil Barracks until 1947, from whence it moved to the Suez Canal. With the Americans, it is represented by the American embassy fortress, also in downtown Cairo, with all streets leading to it blocked and encircled by a phalanx of security forces.

In 1950 Egyptians did rebel and brought the Wafd party to power, which had been representing them well, and the Egyptian government found the temerity to say no to the British by announcing the abrogation of the 1936 Anglo–Egyptian Treaty by unilateral decree. This treaty had been imposed by the British upon Egypt by force. The Wafd government went as far as distributing arms to freedom fighters to stand against the British along the Suez Canal. In January 1952 a group of Egyptian police officers in Ismailiya rebelled, in their turn saying no to the British by disobeying their orders, and the Egyptian government was courageous enough to support this patriotic group.

To this day we do not know the truth behind the Cairo fire in 1952; but we do know that the British, whether they started the fire or not, forced the king to disband the nationalist Wafd government immediately after the blaze and then to bring in one minority government after another, putting an end to the action of the freedom fighters against British forces along the Canal. With the coming of the revolution of July 1952, Egypt was able to defy the British again, this time successfully, and they were compelled to withdraw in 1956.

When Nasser came to be so bold as to say no to the British in 1956 by nationalizing the Suez Canal, and the British threatened to punish Egypt for such rebelliousness, a delegation representing the clique through whom the British had been ruling Egypt before the revolution came to Nasser to tell him that challenging the British was reckless and dangerous, and that it was in the national interest that Nasser should give in to the British and do as he was told. They also told Nasser that Egypt would not be able to manage the Suez Canal efficiently enough. The story goes that Nasser had them put in jail until the Suez Canal crisis was over, with Nasser victorious and the Egyptians having demonstrated that the efficient management of the Canal does not require a miracle. In the same way we can now say to the Americans that for Egypt to realize rapid economic development without American economic aid does not require a miracle. Why is it, then, that Nasser managed to get away with saying no to the British in the 1950s, while we cannot say no to the Americans now?

2

The answer to this question highlights two important differences between the two cases. One has to do with the differences between the international circumstances prevailing at the time of the nationalization of the Suez Canal in 1956 and those prevailing today. The British and the French, whom Nasser challenged in 1956, were experiencing a decline both economically and politically. It did not take long for two new superpowers to take their place and inherit their possessions. These two ascendant players, the United States and the Soviet Union, played a major role in supporting Egyptian defiance of the two declining powers. Indeed, it is possible to view the British and French attack on Egypt (together with Israel) as an indication of weakness rather than strength, as if the two states were making a vain attempt to prove to the world—and perhaps even to themselves—that they were still able to protect their interests by force. This is very different from the case of the United States today. America emerged in the aftermath of the Cold War at the end of the 1980s with no apparent rival. Without any external source of support, how can Egypt say no to the United States today?

The second difference has to do with the social and psychological conditions of the Egyptian people. The Egyptian population in 1956 was no more than twenty-five million, three quarters of whom worked in agriculture. The middle class could not have exceeded one quarter of the population. In the following half-century the population increased threefold to seventy-five million, and the middle class grew to comprise nearly half the population. More important for our purposes is the change that has occurred in the characteristics of the Egyptian middle class. The middle class in Egypt in 1956, despite its small size, was more politicized than it is now. Indeed, it bore much stronger patriotic sentiments and a much greater willingness to make sacrifices in the national cause, as I have tried to show in an earlier chapter. It was certainly much more likely for the Egyptian middle class of the mid-1950s to sympathize with a national leader who said no to the dominant foreign power than now. Turning from mere sympathy to positive action, the contrast between the two periods would be far greater.

In light of the changes that have occurred in both international and domestic circumstances, what should we expect from those holding the reins of power domestically, that is, those who are ruling the country by proxy? The easiest way for them to justify their submission to foreign power is to say that the prevailing international circumstances do not allow them any other course of action. Nevertheless, one thing that makes them bold enough to take such a stand is their awareness of the degree to which people are preoccupied with other matters.

This analysis of international circumstances and of the social and psychological conditions of the Egyptian people, may, however, be a little too hasty. Further consideration of what may be going on under the surface of both the international situation and Egypt's domestic conditions may lead us to discover no less important similarities between what is going on today and the situation that prevailed in 1956.

It may, indeed, appear now, following the collapse of the Soviet Union and the whole socialist bloc, that the United States is the sole ruler of the world and hence it may seem strange to think that the condition of the U.S. today could have some similarities with that of Britain fifty years ago. But did not Britain and its allies achieve an overwhelming victory over their enemies just ten years previous to its dismal experience in Suez? Might not the United States, despite its overwhelming military superiority at present, be taken by surprise by some unanticipated economic, social, or political problems? Indeed, is not the United States already suffering from a relative decline in its position in the world economy vis-à-vis the rising economies elsewhere, especially in East Asia? I have already referred to the possibility of looking at the severity of the British (and French) aggression against Egypt in 1956 as an indication of weakness and not of strength; may we not also view the American aggression against Iraq in 2003 in the same way? Might not the fierceness of the aggression be a manifestation of weakness and fear as opposed to power?

To turn to Egypt's domestic conditions, the apparent changes in the psychological make-up of the Egyptian middle class that occurred over the last four decades may indeed have bred some negative characteristics that work against national revival, but behind this there may have been some other more positive changes. There had been increasing signs in the last twenty years of the rise of a new generation of middle-class Egyptians, less consumption-oriented and more politically aware, with greater vitality and a stronger sense of patriotism, compared to their parents. What they lacked was the freedom to express themselves politically and intellectually. Once the political barriers that stand between them and the seats of power and decision-making collapse, they can make valuable contributions to national revival. This situation reminds one of the situation which prevailed in Egypt just before the 1952 revolution. For it was that revolution which broke similar barriers that stood in the way of a whole generation of Egyptians, who grew up in the 1930s and 1940s, and made a wonderful contribution to the economic, social, and intellectual life of the country in the 1950s and most of the 1960s.

Notes

1 G. Myrdal, *The Challenge of World Poverty*. London: Penguin Press, 1970.

2 Cited in Gamal Hamdan, *The Egyptian Personality*, vol. 2, p. 541. 'Alam al-Kutub, 1981.

3 A system of burdensome tax farming by private contractors eventually abolished by Muhammad 'Ali early in the nineteenth century.

4 Mustafa al-Nahhas (1879–1965) served in several government posts including seven terms as prime minister between 1938 and 1952.

5 Salah Jahin (1930–86) was a colloquial poet, lyricist, playwright, and screenwriter whose efforts helped to legitimize the use of spoken vernacular Arabic in poetry theretofore considered to be the sole domain of ornate classical Arabic. Some of his poems became emblematic popular songs. 'Abd al-Halim Hafez (1929–77) was an immensely popular singer noted for, among other things, reworking the Arab popular song into shorter, catchier tunes than had previously been its form.

6 Egyptian families, especially those of the middle class, usually require outright home ownership of their daughters' prospective suitors.

7 A cylindrical red felt hat.

8 For depictions of these, see Badawi, al-Said, and Martin Hinds. 1986. *A Dictionary of Egyptian Arabic*. Beirut: Librairie du Liban, Plate F, p. 976.

9 See Badawi and Hinds, *A Dictionary of Egyptian Arabic*, Plate B, p. 972, for similar types of baskets.

10 A distinction is often made in Egyptian discourse between the merely 'educated' (*muta'allim*), regardless of how well, and the 'intellectual' (*muthaqqaf*), with the latter word implying a high degree of literary or scholarly production, or both. Galal Amin is saying more than that the ministers were well-educated; he is also saying that they were cultured, in the somewhat old-fashioned sense of being 'men of letters.'

11 Known as the United Arab Republic, the union between Egypt and Syria lasted from 1958 to 1961.

12 Founding member and first president of the new political party (founded 2004) *al-Ghad* (Tomorrow), who stood for the presidency in the 2005 elections, but was arrested on charges of forging power-of-attorney for signatures on the petitions required to allow him to run and was imprisoned in January of the election year (released in 2009). He nevertheless won an unprecedented 7–13 percent of the vote (depending on who was counting).

13 Former head of the Wafd Party, who garnered 3 percent of the vote, but who was then disgraced by violent disputes that broke out outside of party headquarters over a power struggle for leadership of the party.